CITYSCAPES

Cities depend on the strengths and skills of the people who live and work there.

SCHOLASTIC

LITERACY
PLACE®

Copyright acknowledgments and credits appear on page 144, which constitutes an extension of this copyright page.

Copyright ©1996 by Scholastic Inc.   All rights reserved.   Printed in the U.S.A.
                                            ISBN 0-590-49192-X
                  5 6 7 8 9 10   24   02 01 00 99 98 97

Visit an
Urban Planner's Office

Cities depend on the strengths and skills of the people who live and work there.

Touring America's Cities

The people and places of a city give it an identity.

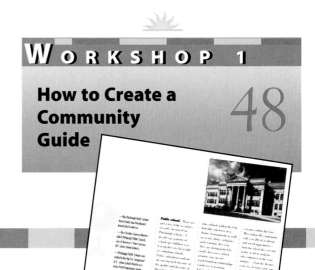

City Challenges

Cities face many complex challenges.

CUSTOMER SATISFACTION SURVEY

Cornerstone Pool is an aquatics pool facility located at 55 Buena Vista Road in West Hartford. The town is considering making changes and improvements to Cornerstone Pool. We are conducting a survey of the people who use Cornerstone Pool to see how you feel about the facility and what changes you would want to see at the facility. Your input is important! When you turn in a completed survey, you will be given a free guest pass to Cornerstone. This is our way of saying thanks for taking the time to complete the survey.

1. How many visits a month on the average do you make to Cornerstone Pool?

2. Please rank in order of importance (1, 2, 3) the 3 reasons you swim at Cornerstone Pool.

    Price is reasonable   Like the programs offered

    Convenient location   Other (please specify)

3. Please rank in order of frequency (1, 2, 3) the three programs you participate in most:

    Youth instructional lessons

Reaching Out

City dwellers can work together to improve their quality of life.

Trade Books

The following books accompany this *Cityscapes* SourceBook.

Social Studies Nonfiction

Cities

by Fiona MacDonald

Fiction

A Jar of Dreams

by Yoshiko Uchida

AWARD WINNING Book

Fiction

Tails of the Bronx

by Jill Pinkwater

AWARD WINNING Author

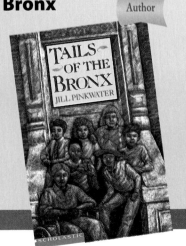

Photo Essay

Where the River Runs

by Nancy Price Graff photographs by Richard Howard

AWARD WINNING Book

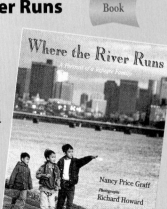

The City By The Golden Gate
© Wooster Scott

Touring America's Cities

Explore San Francisco and discover what makes it special. Search for facts in a chart about other cities around the country.

Read about Elana Rose Rosen, who's just moved into a city apartment building. Look at cities from a poet's point of view, and examine a painting by a famous city artist.

WORKSHOP 1

Create a guide to the biggest and best things about a place you know.

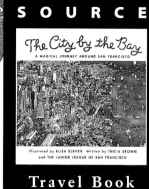
FROM

The City by the Bay

A MAGICAL JOURNEY AROUND SAN FRANCISCO

By **TRICIA BROWN**
and **THE JUNIOR LEAGUE OF SAN FRANCISCO**
Illustrated by **ELISA KLEVEN**

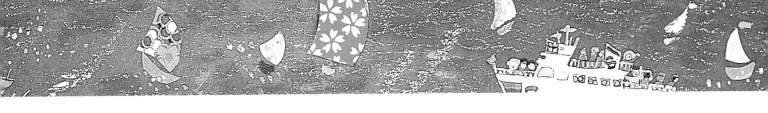

For centuries, perhaps millennia, San Francisco and its Bay were known only by native peoples who lived in small communities throughout Central California. Typically, each community had its own distinct language. As a result, there was never a common name used for the population as a whole.

When the Spanish arrived, they called the natives *costeros,* or "coast people." Later, the English-speaking settlers referred to them as *Costanoans.* Today, descendants of the early natives generally call themselves *Ohlones.*

In the late 16th century, explorers from around the globe began sailing the waters surrounding the San Francisco peninsula. Since that time, San Francisco's population has been made up of an ever-changing mosaic of cultures.

Chinatown

Gung Hay Fat Choy! That means "Happy New Year!" in Chinese. New Year's is a special time in this neighborhood, the largest Chinese community in the western hemisphere. People wish one another good luck and happiness, and children receive *lai-see*—small red envelopes filled with money.

The holiday is celebrated in January or February, depending on the cycle of the moon. Each year is named after one of the twelve animals in the Chinese zodiac. There are many parades and ceremonies. Lots of firecrackers are set off to scare away evil spirits and bring good fortune.

Chinatown is colorful all year round. Walk down Grant Avenue, with its street lights that look like lanterns and street signs written in Chinese. Look at the fresh vegetables and fruits overflowing out to the sidewalk from the grocery stores. Smell the aromas coming from all the different restaurants. Is it time for *dim sum,* a Chinese lunch?

The Cable Cars and Lombard Street

Before 1922, the famous crooked block of Lombard Street was straight, and so steep that it could not be traveled by carts or wagons. The only way for people to get up and down the hill was on foot. After the invention of the automobile, the city added eight turns so that cars would be able to travel the street as well. Today, tourists wait in line to drive down this twisting street.

Visitors can also view Lombard Street from the cable car that runs along Hyde Street. Andrew Hallidie introduced the cable car to San Francisco in 1873 because he felt sorry for the horses pulling wagons up the steep hills. People laughed at his idea at first, but he didn't give up. Today, San Francisco's cable cars are a National Historic Landmark.

The Golden Gate Bridge

Looking from the Marin Headlands to San Francisco on clear evenings, you can watch the twinkling lights of the city, the Golden Gate Bridge, and the San Francisco–Oakland Bay Bridge. On other nights, when the fog rolls in, you can hear the foghorns, and feel the cool fog as it wraps around the Golden Gate Bridge like a blanket.

Although the name of this bridge is the Golden Gate, the paint used to cover it is actually "International Orange." The bridge is named after the strait at the bay's entrance—the Golden Gate.

Some people believed that a bridge could never be built across the Golden Gate, but a group of determined engineers found a way. Built in 1937, the bridge spans a length of 6,450 feet—that's longer than twenty football fields! The tallest tower is 746 feet high—as tall as a 70-story building. The amount of wire used for the main cable is enough to wrap three times around the earth.

17

The Palace of Fine Arts

Although it was originally intended as a temporary exhibit for the 1915 Panama-Pacific Exhibition, the Palace of Fine Arts was so well-loved that it was later rebuilt to become a permanent part of San Francisco's skyline. The beauty of this graceful palace is reflected in a natural lagoon, which is bordered by lawns and trees. The sight is especially stunning at night when the palace is spectacularly lighted. It's a wonderful place to take a stroll, to have a picnic, or to feed the swans and ducks.

The palace is a majestic domed rotunda, with six supporting columns, that is as tall as an eighteen-story building. The angel sculptures inside the rotunda are twenty feet tall. If you want to get an idea of how big that is, you can go into the neighboring Exploratorium and stand next to one of the original angels from the 1915 exhibition!

Fun Facts about the

Lighthouses, foghorns, and buoys guide ships as they navigate San Francisco Bay. Mariners identify the different foghorns by the length and frequency of their "blasts" and the length of the pauses between blasts.

· · · · · · · · · · · · · · · · ·

There are eleven islands within San Francisco's city limits: Angel Island, Yerba Buena, Alcatraz, Treasure Island, and the Farallones (a group of seven islands outside the Golden Gate).

· · · · · · · · · · · · · · · · ·

The Bay Bridge's deepest pier drops 242 feet into the water. Its tallest tower (from bedrock, below the Bay, to the very top) measures nearly 550 feet, making it taller than the largest of the Egyptian pyramids.

San Francisco Bay is not really a bay at all—it's an estuary. (A bay is filled with ocean water. An estuary is filled with a combination of salt water and fresh water.) It is the largest estuary on the west coast of the United States, and has one of the most diverse populations of marine life in the world.

Sutro Tower, San Francisco's tallest structure, transmits television and radio signals from the top of Mt. Sutro.

In 1850, when sourdough bread was delivered to San Franciscans, loaves were placed on spikes outside the doors so that animals could not reach them. Sourdough bread is unique to San Francisco—the wild yeast that is used to make it rise won't grow anywhere else!

· · · · · · · · · · · · · · · · ·

San Francisco has more than 3,000 restaurants.

· · · · · · · · · · · · · · · · ·

The Bay Bridge is actually made up of four bridges: two suspension bridges on the San Francisco side, and a cantilever bridge and a truss bridge on the Oakland side. The two pairs of bridges are connected by a tunnel through Yerba Buena Island.

City by the Bay...

"BART" stands for Bay Area Rapid Transit, the computer-operated, electric-rail train system that connects San Francisco with the East Bay and the Peninsula.

BART's Transbay Tube is 3.6 miles long and rests on the Bay floor, 135 feet beneath the surface of the water. It is made up of 57 giant steel and concrete sections.

Chocolate was not the first product to be manufactured at Ghirardelli Square—it was originally the site of the Pioneer Woolen Mill, which produced uniforms and blankets for the Union Army during the Civil War.

The San Francisco Ballet is the oldest ballet company in America. Founded in 1933, it was the first American ballet company to perform "Nutcracker" and "Swan Lake."

Cable cars are pulled along by underground cables that are constantly moving. A gripman pulls a lever that grips the cable through a slot in the street. When the gripman lets go, a brakeman stops the cable car with wheel and track brakes. The gripman and brakeman ring bells to tell each other when to brake (stop) or grip (go).

San Francisco's firefighters locate emergency water reserves by looking for circles on the streets. 151 intersections have large circles of bricks set into the pavement—each marks a reserve tank holding about 75,000 gallons of water.

Abandoned sailing ships from the Gold Rush days lie buried beneath the streets of San Francisco. The ships were covered by landfill during the city's early days of expansion.

Cities at a Glance

According to the 1990 census, over half the U.S. population lives in cities. Cities around the country have to make sure they can accommodate the growing number of new citizens. This chart shows how the two largest cities from each region of the country meet the needs of their residents.

Northwest

Far West

Midwest

Northeast

Southwest

Southeast

	NORTHEAST		SOUTHEAST	
	NEW YORK	PHILADELPHIA	JACKSONVILLE	MEMPHIS
POPULATION	7,323,000	1,600,000	672,971	610,000
GETTING AROUND	Three subway systems run 230 miles in the city.	Trains connect the city to its suburbs.	Mass transit takes a back seat to cars here.	The city bus and the Main Street Trolley
FAVORITE SPORTS TEAM	Basketball's Knicks and baseball's Yankees	Baseball's Phillies	The Jacksonville Jaguars football team	The Memphis State University Tigers basketball team
MOST RECOGNIZABLE FEATURE	The Statue of Liberty	The Liberty Bell	Jacksonville Landing, a horseshoe-shaped marketplace	The Pyramid, a multipurpose arena that seats 22,500 spectators
LARGEST NEWSPAPER	*The New York Times:* circulation 1,141,366	*The Philadelphia Inquirer:* circulation 486,000	*The Florida Times-Union:* circulation 181,593	*The Commercial Appeal:* circulation 218,000
CITY HELPERS	Teenagers in the City Volunteer Corps help with city events and services.	Action AIDS helps people with the HIV virus.	Volunteer Jacksonville serves the city's many needs.	The Metropolitan Inter-Faith Association uses 3,000 volunteers.
WHERE TO VISIT	The Empire State Building	The Liberty Bell	Twenty miles of white, sandy beaches	Graceland, the home of Elvis Presley
MAJOR INDUSTRIES	Manufacturing, trade, and finance	Banking, insurance, healthcare, and education	Banking and insurance	Education, transportation, and communication
WHERE IT IS	New York	Pennsylvania	Florida	Tennessee

23

	MIDWEST		NORTHWEST	
	CHICAGO	**DETROIT**	**SEATTLE**	**PORTLAND**
POPULATION	2,783,726	1,028,000	516,000	437,319
GETTING AROUND	Bus and rail systems make 1.8 million trips daily.	A car is a must in the motor city.	The Washington State Ferry System is the largest in the U.S.A.	The MAX (Metropolitan Area Express) — a light-rail system
FAVORITE SPORTS TEAM	The Bulls basketball team, baseball's Cubs, and football's Bears	Baseball's Tigers and Hockey's Detroit Red Wings	Basketball's Supersonics and football's Seahawks	Basketball's Portland Trail Blazers
MOST RECOGNIZABLE FEATURE	The Sears Tower, the tallest building in the world	The Renaissance Center, the tallest hotel in North America	The Space Needle, a tower with a revolving restaurant on top	The beautiful snow-capped peaks of Mt. Hood
LARGEST NEWSPAPER	*The Chicago Tribune:* circulation 697,349	*The Detroit Free Press:* circulation 556,116	*The Seattle Times:* circulation 238,600	*The Oregonian:* circulation 348,000
CITY HELPERS	The Children's Home and Aid Society of Illinois helps children and teenagers.	The Detroit Grand Prix Association volunteers at the huge annual auto race.	Patrons of Northwest Civic Cultural and Charitable Organizations raise money for the arts.	The Royal Rosarians pitch in for Portland's famous annual Rose Festival.
WHERE TO VISIT	The Lincoln Park Zoo	The Motown Museum	Pike Place Market, where merchants throw fish to customers	The Oregon Museum of Science and Industry
MAJOR INDUSTRIES	The service industry (workers who do things for others)	Automobile manufacturing and related industries	Aerospace	Timber and manufacturing
WHERE IT IS	Illinois	Michigan	Washington	Oregon

	SOUTHWEST		FAR WEST	
	HOUSTON	**DALLAS**	**LOS ANGELES**	**SAN FRANCISCO**
POPULATION	1,600,000	1,006,877	3,485,398	724,000
GETTING AROUND	Because Houston is spread out over many miles, the most popular form of transit is the car.	DART— Dallas Area Rapid Transit	The new metro system provides a new way to get around LA.	Cable cars provide a picturesque way to get from here to there.
FAVORITE SPORTS TEAM	Basketball's Rockets and football's Oilers	Football's Dallas Cowboys	Basketball's Lakers and baseball's Dodgers compete for fans.	Football's Forty-Niners
MOST RECOGNIZABLE FEATURE	The Astrodome, the first domed stadium ever built	Reunion Tower, a tall, skinny building with a big ball on top	The Hollywood sign sits high in the Hollywood Hills. HOLLYWOOD	The Golden Gate Bridge
LARGEST NEWSPAPER	*The Houston Chronicle:* circulation 417,459	*The Dallas Morning News:* circulation 527,387	*Los Angeles Times:* circulation 1,090,000	*The San Francisco Chronicle:* circulation 526,824
CITY HELPERS	The Green Houston organization supplies fresh produce for soup kitchens.	Big Brothers/Big Sisters pairs adults with kids from single-parent families.	The Tree People plant and maintain city trees.	The St. Anthony Foundation serves San Francisco's inner city.
WHERE TO VISIT	Astroworld amusement park and Galveston Island	The School Book Depository, from which Lee Harvey Oswald shot President Kennedy	Beverly Hills and Universal Studios	Oceanfront Fisherman's Wharf and Pier 39
MAJOR INDUSTRIES	Oil and gas	Financial services — banks, investing, etc.	Entertainment, finance, and tourism	Tourism. This is the most popular destination in the world.
WHERE IT IS	Texas	Texas	California	California

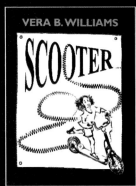

From

By
VERA B. WILLIAMS

When Elana Rose Rosen first moved to 514 Melon Hill, Apartment 8E, the first thing she unpacked was her scooter. For the first few days she leaned on her scooter and looked out the window of her new apartment at the people in the city below. One day, her mom pushed Elana and her scooter out the apartment door, into the elevator, through the lobby, and out the front door and said, "See you at supper time."

SCOOTER
CAN'T YOU
OPEN THE DOOR?
OPEN THAT FRONT DOOR!
TAKE
ELANA OUT....
RIDE AND RIDE___

I pushed on into the courtyard. It was bright and blurry.
Sun bounced off the chrome of my scooter.

Outside our building, 514, and between the other
Melon Hill buildings, there's a long sidewalk. It's great to
ride on. The very first day my mom brought me here, when
the trailer was being unloaded, I watched the other kids
riding bikes there. There's a really smooth cement ramp. It
has wide, flat steps that make a drop just right to jump the
scooter.

I was practicing jumping my scooter. I could already
even it up fast on the straightaway so there was no wobble.
Then I started practicing my double heel click. That's a very
special trick I invented. You have to have good balance to
try it. And you have to have lots of room, so don't try it on a

short runway. Get going fast. Then lean with all your might on the handlebars. Let your legs go way up in back and knock them together fast as you can. Then knock them together again. Simple? It's truly a beautiful trick. I've since even learned to do a triple heel click. But I bet nobody can do a quadruple.

Of course, you do have to have a good scooter. Mine has great balance on account of it has such tremendous wheels. It's beautiful, too. The wheels have a wide silver line all around and a skinny blue stripe like a ribbon around the silver.

Mostly then I was practicing jumps. They were spectacular. After supper my mom came down to watch. It stayed light late then. High up between the buildings you could see a piece of sky turning a special blue. I got my mother to sit so she could see me driving right toward her.

I got a quick start, and I was going fast. Then suddenly there was a big loose thing like a whole piece of sidewalk sticking up in front of me. I just didn't see it soon enough. I couldn't jump that fast.

I landed smash on my face. I think my mom screamed. I think she shook me. She grabbed me and ran out to the street with me. Someone helped us get one of those yellow taxis and told the driver the name of the hospital to take me to.

In the cab I held on to my mother. I was scared of all the blood. I was excited, too. I hoped the taxi would go fast like an ambulance. I wished it had a siren.

The taxi bounced a lot. My mother held her arm tight around me. She talked and cried. She said at least I didn't lose any of my beautiful teeth. She said I was too wild for my own good. She said she was definitely sending the scooter back to Grandma and Grandpa. That made me cry. I said I would go with it if she sent it back. She said I mustn't cry, it made my chin bleed more. She held more tissues to my chin.

The taxi driver started to talk. He told us how he cut his head real bad falling out of a tree when he was a kid. He said to look at the scar on the back of his head. That man was so kind he wouldn't even let my mom pay. He ran into the emergency room with us to show us the way.

The nurse looked at my head and my chin and said the doctor would take care of me soon. Then I had to wait and wait. The arrow with the word E M E R G E N C Y was made of red, red light that kept moving up the arrow. It looked the way the blood pounding in my head felt. The bottom part of my face was getting stiff and couldn't feel.

There was a man with a bandage on his foot bigger than a basketball, even. My mom said not to stare. You see scary things in the hospital. It smells weird, too.

At last the doctor could sew up my cuts. It hurt, and I felt like I was going to be sick. I held so tight to my mother's hand that her hand got numb. My mother told the doctor I wouldn't have had this accident if I wasn't always such a wild kid on my scooter. She told the doctor I was so wild she didn't know what to do with me.

The doctor told my mother not to worry. It wasn't really such a bad accident for a stunt rider. She said I mustn't fall on my head again, though. She bandaged my chin extra thick. When she showed me my face in the mirror, the bandage looked tremendous. I loved the doctor.

I wanted to ride home in a taxi. I liked that taxi driver. My mom said we'd never get the same taxi again. And the bus came right then. I was so sleepy riding home in the bus that the red and green and yellow lights swam together. People's heads swam together. I can't even remember how I got into my bed. I still ask my mother, "But how did I get all the way up in the elevator and undressed and everything, and I didn't even know?"

Way later I woke up. It was in the middle of the middle of the night. I couldn't see. I couldn't tell . . . was I in my grandpa and grandma's house? Was I in our old house with my father before he moved away? Were we still staying at my cousin Nanette's apartment, so full of my cousins' beds you could hardly walk? But on my cousins' street the streetcar went by all night long. How come I couldn't hear the streetcar? Why was there a big lumpy thing on my chin and on my head? And where was my scooter? <u>Where was my scooter?</u>

My mother says she just flew to me when she heard me yelling for my scooter.

She switched on the lights. On the wall between the windows, the funny little light made to look like a candle came on. There was my scooter right in the place I had made for it by the window. I stood on it and looked way down into the streets below. It was raining and the streets were black and wet. I thought I could see the bump that had tripped up my scooter.

"How did my scooter get back up here?" I asked my mother. She told me I was pretty lucky for such a reckless kid. One of our new neighbors, a little boy, Petey, had picked it up and set it by our door. There was just some mud on the wheels and stuff.

"What did he say?" I asked.

"Nothing," my mom said. "He just brought it and stood there...wouldn't say a word. Then he went away."

My mom made us cocoa. I had to drink it in little sips. I tried a cookie, but the bandage made it hard to chew. We sat wrapped up in blankets in the kitchen. Our bathrobes seemed to have disappeared when we moved. My mom says if we have to keep moving finally everything will get lost. Boxes from our dishes were still around us. You never saw so many boxes as when you move. My mom just couldn't wait till she got enough time to get rid of all the boxes. But I liked it. It felt as if we were camping.

Our big blue pot with speckles and our frying pan and our toaster were sitting around the legs of my chair. I told my mom that the big blue pot was asking the frying pan and the toaster how they liked their new kitchen.

My mom said she thought the big blue pot was saying how glad it was that I was okay, and the toaster was saying how it hoped I would be able to eat toast real soon. I laughed, but that hurt my chin, too. Then I took my cocoa to my bed.

But I didn't even get back in my bed. I found a rag so I could clean every bit of mud off my scooter. I looked through the boxes and found the one marked F I X . I got the little squirt can of oil out. I oiled the wheels. Then I polished and I polished the silver stripe with the blue stripe like a ribbon around it till I made those stripes so bright you could even see them in the dark.

FRIENDS
REALLY ARE
IMPORTANT,
ESPECIALLY
NICE FRIENDS.
DIFFICULT FRIENDS
SOMETIMES ARE GREAT TOO.

The day after the day after my accident I had to wait in the elevator a long time on seven. A lady was holding the door for her friend, who had run back to her apartment to unplug her iron even though <u>everybody</u> thought it wasn't fair to hold the elevator that long. I was telling Cecelia from right next door about my ride to the hospital. Then this kid ran into the elevator, saw it wasn't going anywhere and ran out, ducked back in, and pulled me out down the hall with him.

"You know me, I'm Jimmy Beck right under you in 7E. Listen, I'll show you how we get down fast in this building." He pushed open the heavy door to the fire stairs.

"I guess you know everything," I said, to be sarcastic. It's the meanest way I know to be, since I can't stand when people make sarcastic remarks to me. But it didn't bother him. He was leaping the steps from the seventh floor to the sixth in bunches. When I caught up with him on the landing, he was writing hard into the skin of his arm with a ballpoint: J.B. KNOWS EVERYTHING.

"Jimmy Beck knows everything," he sang, running down the stairs to five. I love to run and jump down stairs fast, too, and I wanted to see this back part of our building and where we'd come out. Only I couldn't run now. It made my head hurt. So Jimmy got to all the landings first. He jumped the last half of each flight and ran back up so he wouldn't ever have to stop talking.

From the fifth to the fourth, he told me Eduard with the skateboard lived in 4K and the scooter tricks he saw me doing were almost as good as Eduard's skateboard stuff. For a girl, that is, he added.

From the fourth to the third, he explained that he didn't get a skateboard because he got a fifteen-speed instead, and did I know a kid named Vinh on the third floor?

From the third to the second, he told me he knew day before yesterday I was going to wreck up on that piece of broken pavement, and he had yelled at me to watch out, but I was too stuck-up to listen.

On the second, he stood still (sort of) to tell me he had once had an accident standing on a swing going over the top, and blood ran out his nose and his mouth and his ears and his eyes just like the Mississippi. Running again, he pointed down the hall and said a dumb little kid named Petey lived there. He made a sign with his finger that Petey was crazy.

On the first floor, he said Adrienne lived down the hall and her parents owned the variety store only they charged way too much for everything.

We finally pushed open the fire door to the outside. "C'mon," Jimmy called, racing for the courtyard. But I had

had enough of Jimmy Beck, so I took my time. I wanted to explore every bit of Melon Hill Houses. There were two playgrounds and tables for games, I knew, but I had the feeling there was lots more to find than I had noticed right off.

I met a lot of kids that day and the next. And it was partly thanks to Jimmy Beck's big mouth, I have to admit. Kids had heard about my accident, about lots of blood (<u>much</u> more than there was) and about a scooter that had huge silver and blue wheels and maybe you could get rides on.

I'm not at all sure Jimmy Beck can be what I call a friend. But Vinh or Eduard or Adrienne will be. All three of us might do a lot of things together. They're all in the same class in the school where I'll be going. I'll be in their class, too, after the summer when we start school.

Siobhan and Beryl are in other classes. Beryl wears lipstick already, and she likes to act sexy. And Adrienne from the first floor, her mother is going to have a baby real soon. Eduard's like me with my scooter. Only he's much more of a single-minded person than I am about wheels. He <u>never</u> goes out without his skateboard. He even rides it in the halls. We're not allowed to ride in the halls. But you should see how he can come right up to the elevator door, then stop in one little inch!

Then there's Petey. I've heard the kids say things about Petey. He's the little kid who brought home my scooter after my accident. I haven't met him yet, but I know he lives in my building and I know where. I bet it won't be long, either, till I know every kid in this building. But I am especially curious about Petey.

LOOK
UP, LOOK DOWN, LOOK ALL AROUND
CAN'T EVER
KNOW FOR SURE
YOUR LUCKY DAY!

A few days after my accident Adrienne rang our bell. She wanted to see the bandage on my head. She was never even in an apartment on the eighth floor before. She said she liked standing up on the scooter and looking out the window.

"I'd be so scared to live here, Lanny," she said. "You're almost to the roof." She didn't really like it. She's used to the first floor. Only she got excited when she found Thieu's Variety Store. That's her parents' store. Then she saw our school. "You can see pretty much from up here," she said.

She asked me where I slept, so I showed her my couch. Anyone can tell it's mine because mine is on my side of our big room right by my scooter. It has the cover with the rosy flowers. My mom's has the cover with brown and blue flowers, and the rug is in between. And mine has my old bear and my lion on it. I wanted my own room so bad, but my mom said it would be quite awhile before she could afford that. When I suggested she ask my father for money for more rent, she said, like she usually does, "Put <u>that</u> out of your mind, honey!" (But I never <u>really</u> do.)

Adrienne said I needed to get a screen like she has to separate her bed from her little brother's bed. She said their apartment has two rooms besides the kitchen, but her mom and dad had one whole room and she and her brother shared the little room. Then her uncle made a screen for her and that was much better. She took me down to show her mother my bandage.

Her mother said she was so sad that my head was hurt. She said my hair was very pretty and it would grow back nice where they had to cut it for the bandage. Then she said I shouldn't ride that scooter anymore and how my mother should know what a bad toy that scooter is for a young girl. She was really upset about that and went on talking about it to herself and shaking her head. Adrienne showed me her own bed with the screen around it. It was almost better than a real door. It made it look private and secret and cozy. I decided I was going to have a screen like that around my bed, too.

We kneeled on Adrienne's bed and leaned on her windowsill. You can actually talk to people and see everything just like you're down in the street. We could see our super, Benny Portelli, helping the man who drives the special big white truck. The truck only comes on Fridays to take away old furniture no one wants anymore.

And then my special thing happened to me. Suddenly I got lucky again! My mother says the fairies must have come when I was born, just like in the story, to bring me their special gifts. She says one of them must have brought me good luck, because over and over anyone can see that I'm one really lucky kid.

And I am, too. At that very minute Mr. Portelli was handing a screen to the garbageman in the back of the truck. It looked a lot like Adrienne's screen, with wood all around like a picture frame and red cloth.

"Wait . . . Wait, Benny . . . Mr. Portelli! Wait!" I yelled.

"Excuse me!" I yelled to Mrs. Thieu. I had to really race through their kitchen.

"Your head!" Mrs. Thieu called after me. "Your head!"

I could feel my bandage sliding down over my eyes, but I ran right over to Benny.

"Mr. Portelli!" I remembered my mom said I should say "Mr. Portelli." "Don't throw away that screen. Please. Please, I need it."

"You want it?" He held it out to me. "It's yours. Just don't let me find it out here tomorrow."

Adrienne came down to help me take it up to my house. It was not an old thing at all. There was nothing broken or

torn. It was very dusty, and the wooden frame was scrappy looking. Adrienne helped me clean it all up. I set it around my bed. Adrienne said I was an amazingly lucky person.

When my mother came in, she agreed it was the perfect thing. She kept hitting her head and saying she didn't know how come she never even thought of a screen for me.

I told her how I saved it from the garbage truck just in time.

"Because you're lucky," she said. She hugged me. She started to cry. She fussed getting my bandage straight. "You were lucky you didn't break your head," she said, "Elana Rose Rosen."

On Saturday, she took all the cloth off the screen, and I scrubbed it. Then we could see how pretty and bright it really was. She tacked it all back on the frame tight with special new brass upholstery tacks. She sent me to see if Mr. Portelli had a little upholsterer's hammer we could use, and I helped her hammer in the tacks. Then I made my sign.

Every Day She Rides Her Scooter

Loves To Dance And Loves Music

Admits She Acts Stupid And Stuck Up Sometimes

Now She Has Friends At Melon Hill Houses

And Nanette Is Coming

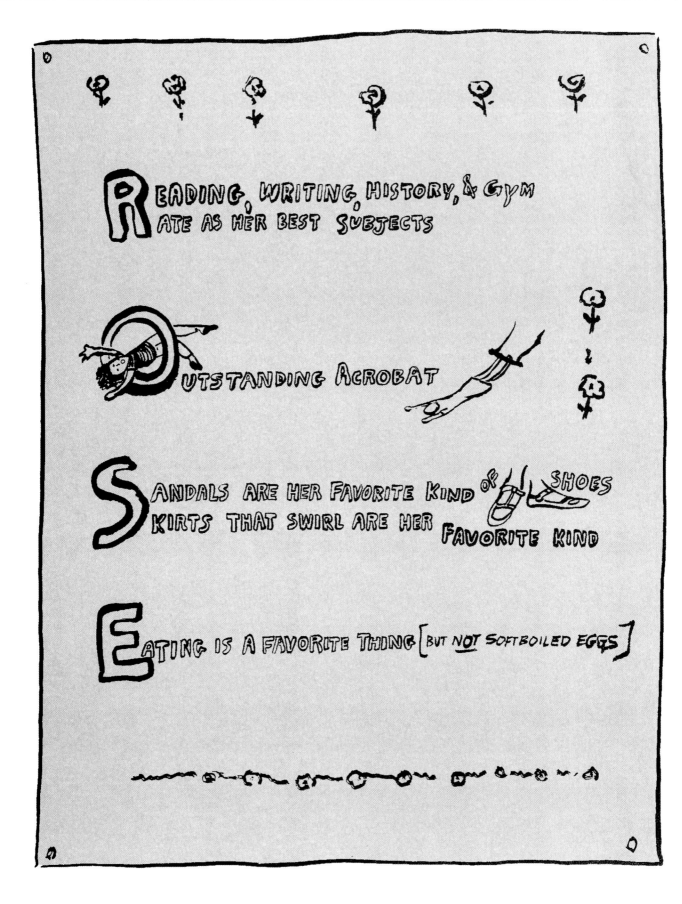

READING, WRITING, HISTORY, & GYM RATE AS HER BEST SUBJECTS

OUTSTANDING ACROBAT

SANDALS ARE HER FAVORITE KIND OF SHOES SKIRTS THAT SWIRL ARE HER FAVORITE KIND

EATING IS A FAVORITE THING [BUT _NOT_ SOFTBOILED EGGS]

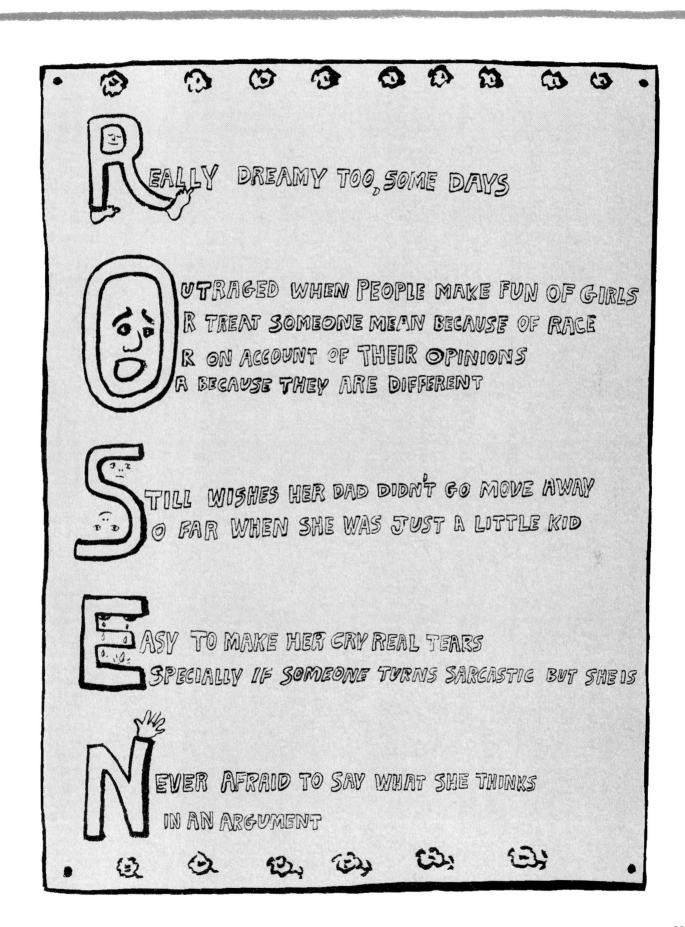

REALLY DREAMY TOO, SOME DAYS

OUTRAGED WHEN PEOPLE MAKE FUN OF GIRLS
R TREAT SOMEONE MEAN BECAUSE OF RACE
R ON ACCOUNT OF THEIR OPINIONS
R BECAUSE THEY ARE DIFFERENT

STILL WISHES HER DAD DIDN'T GO MOVE AWAY
O FAR WHEN SHE WAS JUST A LITTLE KID

EASY TO MAKE HER CRY REAL TEARS
SPECIALLY IF SOMEONE TURNS SARCASTIC BUT SHE IS

NEVER AFRAID TO SAY WHAT SHE THINKS
IN AN ARGUMENT

PETEY IS MY SHADOW!
EVERYWHERE I GO HE GOES TOO.
TALKS NOT AT ALL!
ESPECIALLY FUN TO PLAY WITH.
YOU COULD LOVE HIM LOTS!
YOU COULD GET MAD AT HIM TOO!

A week after my accident, I met Petey for real.

When the elevator door opened to let me out on eight, he was standing there. He followed me to our door. His shoelaces were untied, and he had to stop and wiggle his shoe back on. I waited for him. I was sure he was the little kid who saved my scooter. I thought maybe he was five or four like my twin cousins. But they can tie shoes.

"Can't you tie your shoes?" I asked him. He wouldn't answer. "What's your name?" I asked him. He wouldn't tell me that, either, but he nodded when I said "Petey?" And he nodded again when I asked was he the Petey who saved my scooter. While I was bending over trying to unlock our door, I could feel him touching the bandage on my head. It's just a small bandage now, and the doctor will take out the stitches tomorrow.

He followed me right in. On Tuesdays, my mom doesn't get home from her school and her job till just before supper. I was glad Petey was there. We went and looked at my bandage in the bathroom mirror. I took him in to see the scooter. The handlebars were high for him, but he stood on it just like he was riding it. I showed him the great features of this particular scooter. I held it up a little so he could spin the wheels and watch the silver and blue stripes blur. I let him help me polish them.

He never even said anything the whole time. I asked him if he could talk. He polished very hard but he didn't answer.

Petey came next door to Cecelia's with me. Cecelia is how come we found this apartment. She was a friend of my mom's a long time ago, even before my mom got married. (She even knew my father.) Cecelia works at the supermarket, but only part-time. When my mom gets home late, Cecelia is usually home. I go there, and she gives me a snack. We do puzzles and play Scrabble. She has fish and a big parrot that talks, and she has plants in cans all over the windowsill and hanging up. I am teaching the parrot new words. But Petey was scared of the parrot. Very scared. He stood in the corner and never moved his eyes from that big bird. And he never said anything.

Cecelia told me in the kitchen that as far as she was informed he never did say a word. But she couldn't say for sure if he could or not. She gave us both glasses of cranberry juice and told me where to take Petey back to his baby-sitter, Mrs. Greiner, down at the other stairs on nine. That's how I first met Mrs. Greiner and got a job.

I help Mrs. Greiner take care of Petey. Because he runs and runs, and she complains she's much too slow and much too fat for that. She wears special furry slippers. They don't do much for her because feet such as hers are beyond help, she says. But she finds Petey real smart and quick. "Turn around and he's gone! Turn around again and he's back!" Mrs. Greiner just loves Petey. She's crazy about him. She'd be sad if she couldn't be Petey's baby-sitter. So I do the running after, and she does the looking after. I listen to her complaining. I do errands for her. Besides baby-sitting, she strings beads for people when their necklaces break. And I'm the delivery girl.

Don't think it is an easy thing to restring beads the way they were. It isn't. You have to make a knot between each bead, and each knot has to be in the exact right spot.

Mrs. Greiner tried to teach me, but my knots never came out in the right place. So then she told me she could see that I was meant to be a messenger, <u>not</u> a knitter or a knotter or any of those things.

But she can do all of those things very fast: knit and crochet and embroider and fix broken cups and earrings and carve teeny animals from wood.

And you can't always tell about Mrs. Greiner. When she's busy she won't stop for anything. But when she feels like it she tells long stories about when she was a child. And she has a lot to say about Melon Hill Houses, <u>and</u> the borough <u>and</u> the city <u>and</u> the whole world . . . . But she has a lot of things that hurt her besides her feet, I think. She says when it's hot out she can hardly move and when it's cold her bones can feel it bad. And wind gets to her. And rain. And when the news is bad it puts her off her food.

But she doesn't make good things to eat. Petey doesn't like to eat at Mrs. Greiner's, and neither do I. Petey likes to eat at my house. One time after she had been talking at me the whole morning about Melon Hill Houses not being kept up nice anymore and about things she read out of the newspaper about people who have nowhere to live and about how much fake pearls and those necklace clasps cost . . . I decided I better just go home. She has a special sad voice when she says all those things. It makes me feel <u>I</u>, Elana Rose Rosen, better do something right away about the mayor and the price of beads . . . and housing . . . whatever . . . immediately!

The next time I walked up the stairs to her apartment, I made up a nickname to call her.

REALLY LOVES HER
ELANA RUSE ROSEN
NO WONDER THAT
IS AN UNUSUAL LADY
HAS NO T.V. IN HER HOUSE
WINS AT SCRABBLE MOST TIMES

EVERY SHAPE AND EVERY COLOR
HAS THOUSANDS OF BEADS
TELLS THE GREATEST STORIES

RUMBLES IN HER STOMACH AND WE LAUGH
EATS THINGS SHE SAYS AREN'T GOOD FOR HER
NEVER GIVES UP WHEN HER WOOL TANGLES
IS ALWAYS TALKING POLITICS TO EVERYBODY
ESPECIALLY ADORES PETEY
RAINY DAYS MAKE HER FEET HURT
GUESSES RIDDLES AND GUESSES WHAT'S BOTHERING YOU

SHE CAN JUST FORGET I'M A KID AND NOT A GROWN-UP
REALLY NICE TO ME BUT A LITTLE UNPREDICTABLE TOO
MAKES LUMPY SOUP, BURNED TOAST AND RUNNY EGGS

THE GREATEST CITY

AWARD WINNING

Poet

by Walt Whitman

What do you think endures?
Do you think the greatest city endures?
Or a teeming manufacturing state? or
    a prepared constitution? or the best
    built steamships?
Or hotels of granite and iron? or any
    chef-d'oeuvres of engineering,
    forts, armaments?
Away! These are not to be cherished
    for themselves,
They fill their hour, the dancers dance,
    the musicians play for them,
The show passes, all does well enough
    of course,
All does very well till one flash of defiance.

The greatest city is that which has the
    greatest men and women,
If it be a few ragged huts, it is still the
    greatest city in the whole world.

Study for Grand Central, 1993
Red Grooms
Watercolor on paper, 22½ X 30"
Courtesy, Marlborough Gallery

How to Create a Community Guide

In many cities and towns, municipal organizations publish guides that describe their communities. People who are interested in living or working in a particular place might consult a community guide to learn more about it.

What is a community guide? A community guide helps answer important questions such as: Where will I live? How will I get to work? Where are community schools and hospitals located? A community guide also tells about the special features that make a city or town unique—community events, things to do for fun, and natural resources like beaches or mountains.

Names of the community's nine colleges and universities

Additional information of interest to local professionals

Public school. These are just a few of the accolades recently bestowed on Pittsburgh schools. A decade ago, parents of school-age children were leaving the City for wealthier suburban schools. Today, suburban residents are moving back because of the quality and diversity of the City's schools. For students K-12, Pittsburgh offers comprehensive programs in such subjects as creative and performing arts, international studies, geographic and life sciences, polytechnics, computer science, high technology, law and public service, and teaching as well as general academic programs at neighborhood schools. They also provide early childhood programs, day care, after school care, Head Start, a handicapped preschool and both half-day and full-day kindergartens. Innovative programs such as these have increased Pittsburgh's enrollment … so much so that Pittsburgh Public Schools is one of the few school districts in Allegheny County that is reopening elementary schools.

Private school.
Pittsburgh's private schools are highly regarded. The Independent Schools of Greater Pittsburgh include

nine schools within the City that offer intensive academic environments as well as racial, ethnic, religious and economic diversity. They are distinguished by small class sizes, which promote one-on-one teacher/student relationships conducive to learning. Financial assistance is available to help with tuition, which ranges from $6,000 to $10,000 per year, depending on the school. In addition, the Catholic Diocese operates 29 elementary and middle schools, and four secondary schools within Pittsburgh. They emphasize the religious principles of the Catholic tradition in addition to a progressive academic curriculum. Subsidized by parishioners, the cost of Catholic schooling in Pittsburgh is in the $2,000-a-year range.

Higher education.
Pittsburghers derive enormous benefits through access to the nine colleges and uni-

versities within the City. They infuse the community with a wealth of academic and social opportunity— from the talent they recruit, to the resident students who volunteer in the community … from the theatre, concerts, lectures and symposiums featuring universally known speakers and artists that they sponsor, to the credit and non-credit courses they teach. Pittsburgh's array of postsecondary technical schools, such as the Pittsburgh Art Institute and the Pittsburgh Culinary Institute, also offer unique educational opportunities. Whether you're interested in an M.B.A. or a Ph.D., an elective course in speech writing or skydiving, sending your second grader to college computer camp, or becoming a world class chef, one of Pittsburgh's institutions of higher learning will meet your need.

Pittsburgh Colleges & Universities

Carlow College

Carnegie Mellon University

Chatham College

Community College of Allegheny County

Duquesne University

Pittsburgh Theological Seminary

Point Park College

Robert Morris College

University of Pittsburgh

Fortune has rated Pittsburgh the Eighth Best City for Business and the Fifth Largest Corporate Headquarters City. *Savvy* has named it the Third Most Livable City for Women; *Working Mother* has called it the Second Best City for Working Mothers. All told, Pittsburgh is a good place to grow professionally— for men and women.

Corporate diversity.
Pittsburgh is headquarters to 12 *Fortune* 500 industrial companies, including *Fortune* 100 giants like Westinghouse Electric, H.J. Heinz, USX, Alcoa and PPG, and four *Fortune* 500 service firms. The skyline reflects this corporate prestige— seven skyrise office complexes have opened Downtown since 1980. Pittsburgh's economy is fueled today by health care, education, finance, light manufacturing and service businesses. High technology businesses are also flourishing— Pennsylvania ranks third in the U.S. behind California and Massachusetts in the number of high technology businesses, and

the Pittsburgh region is home to 35 percent of the state's high tech companies. There are nearly 80 companies and 65,000 employees in advanced technology in the Pittsburgh area. More than 170 research centers are located in Pittsburgh, which has one of the highest concentrations of engineers, scientists and technicians in the nation.

Media. Pittsburgh ranks among the Top 20 media markets in the U.S. with eight television stations (including the country's first public television station, WQED-TV) and 33 radio stations (including the nation's first, KDKA-AM). Both a morning and evening daily newspaper as well as an assortment of well-read weekly and monthly publications catering to the business, cultural and multiethnic communities keep Pittsburgh professionals informed.

Networking. Two hundred chapters of national professional organizations, from Toastmasters to the National

Information about the community's schools

Types of companies found in the community

1 Brainstorm

First, choose the community you'd like to create a guide for—either your own or a neighboring city or town. You might also choose a community where you've lived in the past, or a city that you've often visited. Then, brainstorm a list of things about that community that you think people who are moving there would want to know about. It might help to think of different subjects you want to cover in your guide, such as weather, transportation, schools, museums, businesses, neighborhoods, people, things to do, or any other subjects you think are important or interesting.

TOOLS

- paper and pencil
- colored pencils, crayons, or markers
- resource materials

Tip You don't have to stick to information you get from books and pamphlets when you plan your guide. Do you have a favorite place to play ball or ride your skateboard? Or a person in your community you really admire? Including personal information can help others enjoy your city.

2 Research

Review the list of subjects you'd like to include in your guide. Then, decide what kind of information you want to present about each subject. For example, if you'd like to include museums in your guide, you could find out how many museums are in your community, their opening and closing times, what famous things are on display there, and how many people visit them each year. To find the information you need, you might want to check some or all of these sources: a history book about the community, a brochure from the Chamber of Commerce, a map of the city, an almanac or encyclopedia, or a clerk at City Hall.

3 Write Guide Entries

Now that you've researched the subjects, it's time to write your guide. You might want to write a short paragraph describing each entry. Or, you could put the information you've found in list or chart form. Before putting together the final version of your guide, review your entries to make sure you've included all of the information you found. Revise the entries if necessary.

4 Assemble Your Guide

You might want to organize your guide into sections, with such labels as "Places to Go," "Things to Do," and "How to Get Around." Draw pictures or use photos and maps to illustrate the entries in your guide. If you found any quotes about your community, you can include them, too. Create a cover for your guide, using photos of life in your community. When you're finished, share your guide with the class.

If You Are Using a Computer

Use the Newsletter format to write your guide. You can write headlines for each section, then type the entries. Print out and assemble your guide, adding photos, maps, and drawings.

THINK

An urban planner must know a lot about her city. What did you learn about your community that you didn't know before?

Karen Heit
Urban Planner ▶

Cities face many complex challenges.

City Challenges

Read a fantastic
story about a
city whose streets
are overrun by
giant trucks.

Meet urban planner
Karen Heit, who
keeps Los Angeles
on the move.

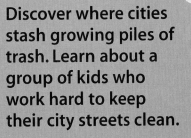

Discover where cities
stash growing piles of
trash. Learn about a
group of kids who
work hard to keep
their city streets clean.

WORKSHOP 2

Conduct a needs assessment to
find out what your community
needs most.

CORNERSTONE POOL

CUSTOMER
SATISFACTION
SURVEY

Cornerstone Pool is an aquatics pool facility located at
55 Buena Vista Road in West Hartford. The town is considering
making changes and improvements to Cornerstone Pool. We are
conducting a survey of the people who use Cornerstone to see how you
feel about the facility and what changes you would want to see at the
facility. Your input is important! When you turn in a completed survey, you
will be given a free guest pass to Cornerstone. This is our way of saying thanks
for taking the time to complete the survey.

1. How many visits a month on the average do you make to Cornerstone Pool?

2. Please rank in order of importance (1, 2, 3) the 3 reasons you swim at Cornerstone Pool.

_____ Price is reasonable   _____ Like the programs offered

_____ Convenient location   _____ Other (please specify)

53

From
THE PUSHCART WAR

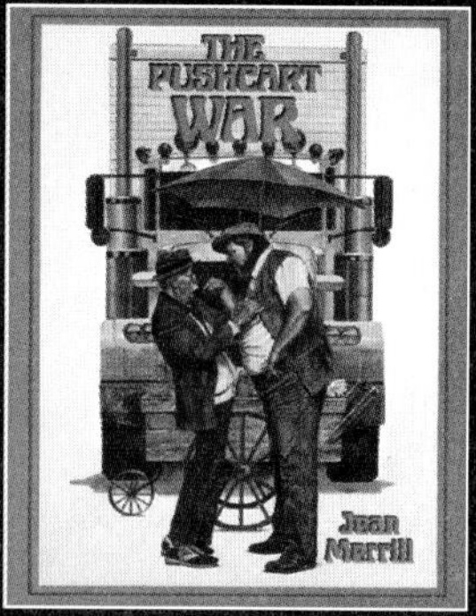

By Jean Merrill
Illustrated by Beata Szpura

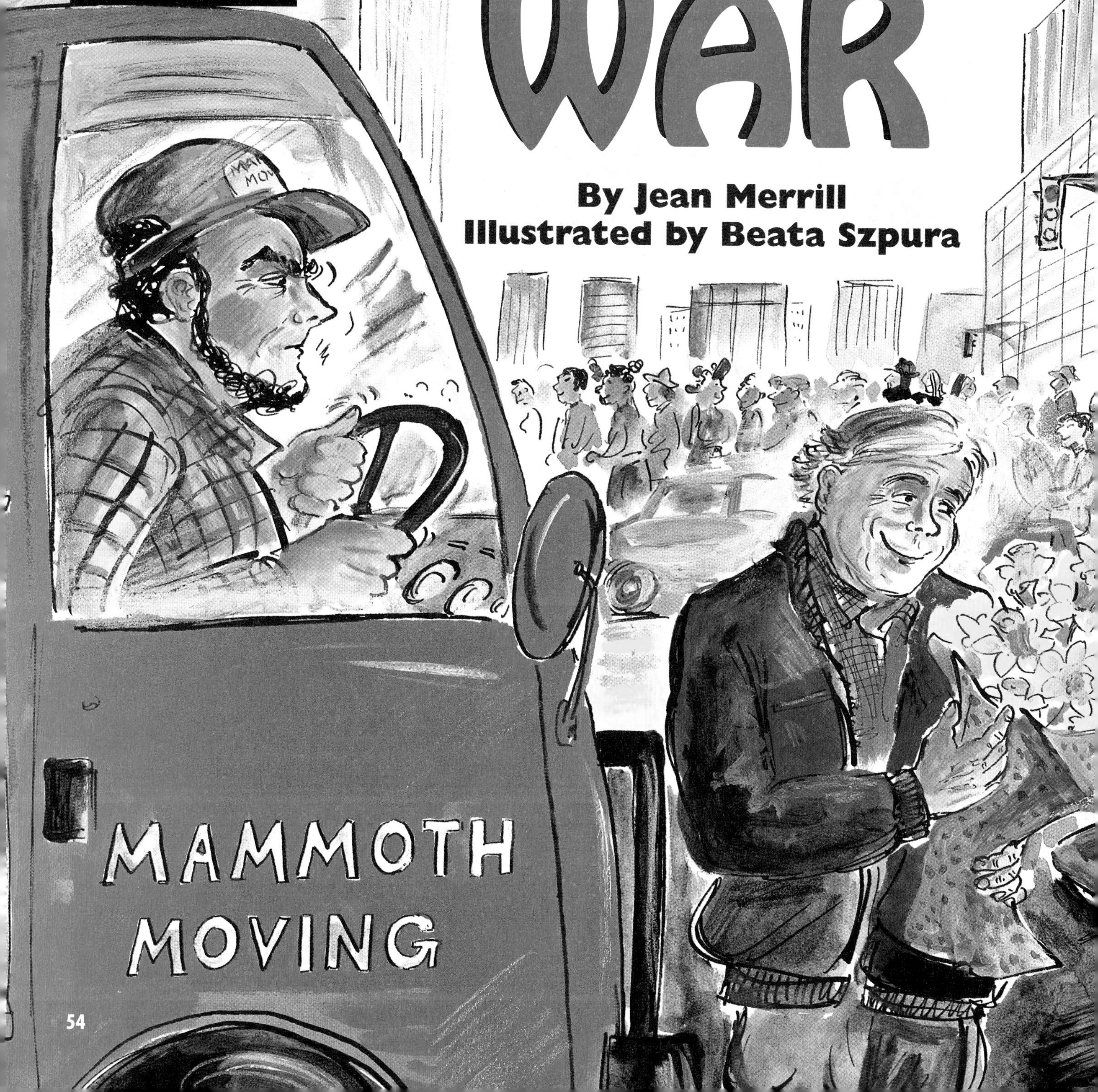

MAMMOTH
MOVING

How It Began: The Daffodil Massacre

The Pushcart War started on the afternoon of March 15, 1998, when a truck ran down a pushcart belonging to a flower peddler. Daffodils were scattered all over the street. The pushcart was flattened, and the owner of the pushcart was pitched headfirst into a pickle barrel.

The owner of the cart was Morris the Florist. The driver of the truck was Mack, who at the time was employed by Mammoth Moving. Mack's full name was Albert P. Mack, but in most accounts of the Pushcart War, he is referred to simply as Mack.

It was near the corner of Sixth Avenue and 17th Street in New York City that the trouble occurred. Mack was trying to park his truck. He had a load of piano stools to deliver, and the space in which he was hoping to park was not quite big enough.

When Mack saw that he could not get his truck into the space by the curb, he yelled at Morris the Florist to move his pushcart. Morris' cart was parked just ahead of Mack.

Morris had been parked in this spot for half an hour, and he was doing a good business. So he paid no attention to Mack.

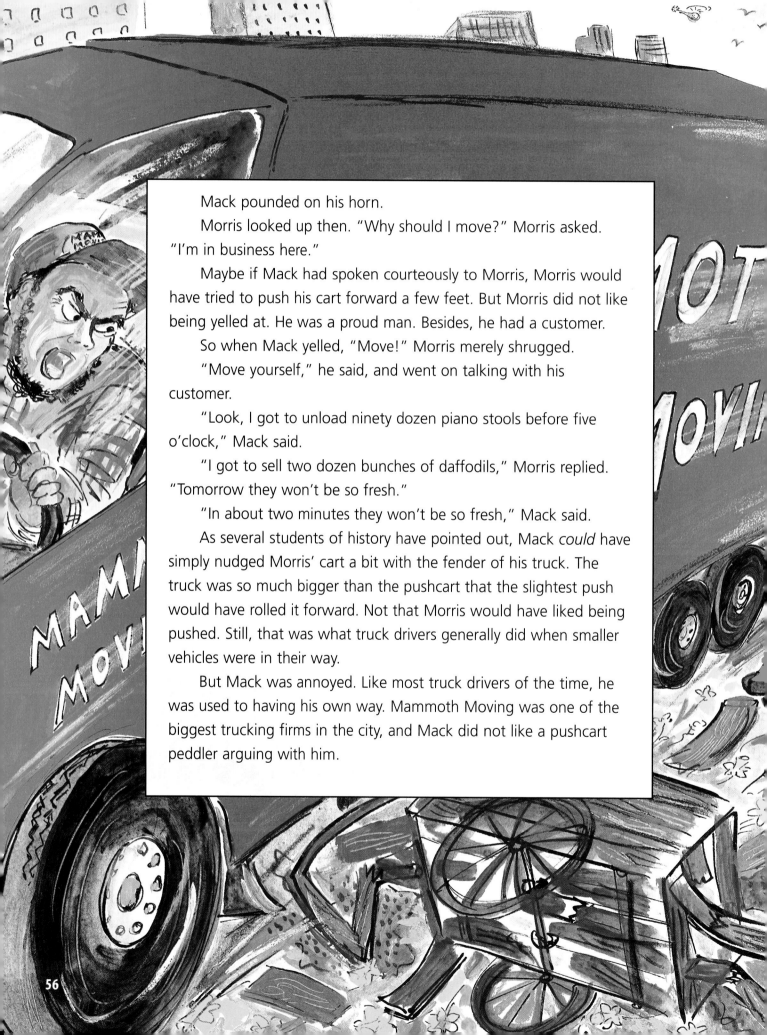

Mack pounded on his horn.

Morris looked up then. "Why should I move?" Morris asked. "I'm in business here."

Maybe if Mack had spoken courteously to Morris, Morris would have tried to push his cart forward a few feet. But Morris did not like being yelled at. He was a proud man. Besides, he had a customer.

So when Mack yelled, "Move!" Morris merely shrugged.

"Move yourself," he said, and went on talking with his customer.

"Look, I got to unload ninety dozen piano stools before five o'clock," Mack said.

"I got to sell two dozen bunches of daffodils," Morris replied. "Tomorrow they won't be so fresh."

"In about two minutes they won't be so fresh," Mack said.

As several students of history have pointed out, Mack *could* have simply nudged Morris' cart a bit with the fender of his truck. The truck was so much bigger than the pushcart that the slightest push would have rolled it forward. Not that Morris would have liked being pushed. Still, that was what truck drivers generally did when smaller vehicles were in their way.

But Mack was annoyed. Like most truck drivers of the time, he was used to having his own way. Mammoth Moving was one of the biggest trucking firms in the city, and Mack did not like a pushcart peddler arguing with him.

When Mack saw that Morris was not going to move, he backed up his truck. Morris heard him gunning his engine, but did not look around. He supposed Mack was going to drive on down the block. But instead of that, Mack drove straight into the back of Morris' pushcart. Daffodils were flung for a hundred feet and Morris himself, as we have said, was knocked into a pickle barrel. This was the event that we now know as the Daffodil Massacre.

These facts about the Daffodil Massacre are known because a boy, who had just been given a camera for his birthday, happened to be standing by the pickle barrel. His name was Marvin Seeley.

The Blow-up of Marvin Seeley's Picture

Marvin Seeley had been trying, on the afternoon of March 15th, to take a picture of a pickle barrel which stood in front of a grocery store on 17th Street. Marvin had been annoyed to have a man go flying into the barrel at the very instant he snapped the picture. However, when the picture was developed, the daffodils came out so nicely that Marvin sent the picture to a magazine that was having a contest.

Although the magazine preferred pictures of plain pickle barrels to pictures of accidents, the picture won an Honorable Mention and was printed in the magazine where a newspaper editor's wife, named Emily Wisser, happened to see it. Emily, who was fond of flowers, cut out the picture for a scrapbook she kept.

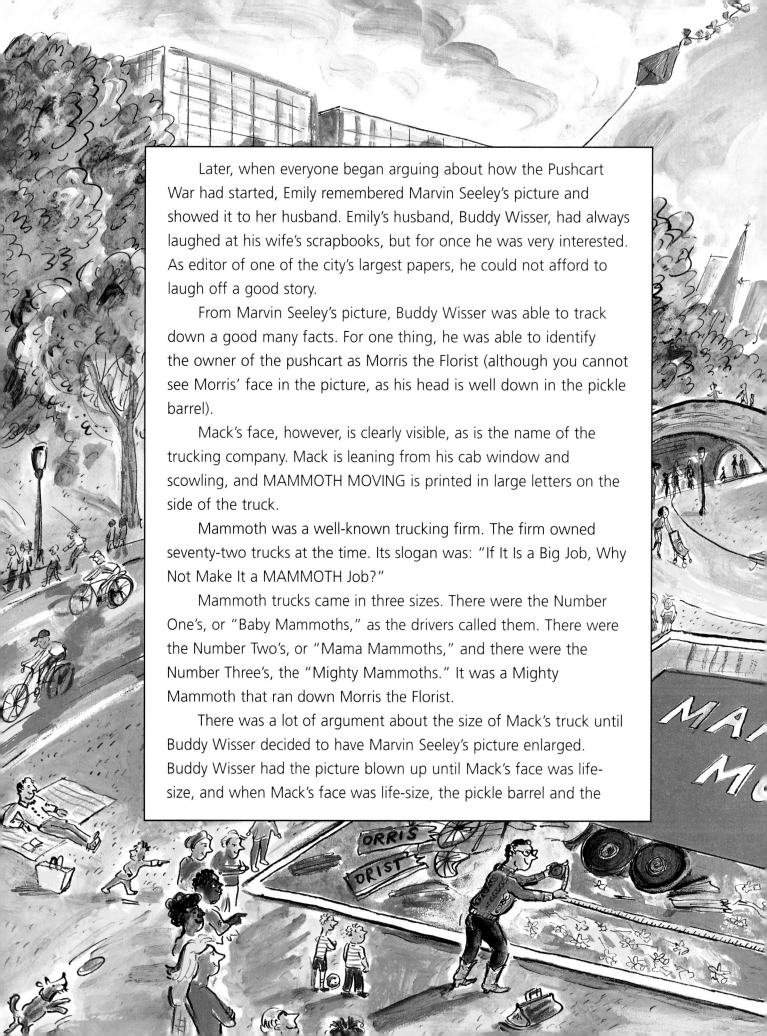

Later, when everyone began arguing about how the Pushcart War had started, Emily remembered Marvin Seeley's picture and showed it to her husband. Emily's husband, Buddy Wisser, had always laughed at his wife's scrapbooks, but for once he was very interested. As editor of one of the city's largest papers, he could not afford to laugh off a good story.

From Marvin Seeley's picture, Buddy Wisser was able to track down a good many facts. For one thing, he was able to identify the owner of the pushcart as Morris the Florist (although you cannot see Morris' face in the picture, as his head is well down in the pickle barrel).

Mack's face, however, is clearly visible, as is the name of the trucking company. Mack is leaning from his cab window and scowling, and MAMMOTH MOVING is printed in large letters on the side of the truck.

Mammoth was a well-known trucking firm. The firm owned seventy-two trucks at the time. Its slogan was: "If It Is a Big Job, Why Not Make It a MAMMOTH Job?"

Mammoth trucks came in three sizes. There were the Number One's, or "Baby Mammoths," as the drivers called them. There were the Number Two's, or "Mama Mammoths," and there were the Number Three's, the "Mighty Mammoths." It was a Mighty Mammoth that ran down Morris the Florist.

There was a lot of argument about the size of Mack's truck until Buddy Wisser decided to have Marvin Seeley's picture enlarged. Buddy Wisser had the picture blown up until Mack's face was life-size, and when Mack's face was life-size, the pickle barrel and the

daffodils and the truck were all life-size, too. Then all Buddy Wisser had to do was to take a tape measure and measure the truck.

Not that this was easy. The enlarged picture was so large that Buddy Wisser had to go to a park near his office and lay the picture on the ground in order to measure the truck. It was a Mighty Mammoth, all right.

It was this big picture that also gave Buddy Wisser the clue he needed to identify the owner of the pushcart. In the lower left-hand corner of the picture, Buddy observed several splintered bits of the pushcart. On one of these fragments, he made out the letters "ORRIS," and on another—"ORIST."

Buddy Wisser's enlargement of Marvin Seeley's picture now hangs in the Museum of the City of New York. The Museum preserved the picture, partly because its size makes it a curiosity, and partly because it is a historical document. It is the best proof we have of how the Pushcart War actually began.

More About Morris the Florist & A Little About Frank the Flower and Maxie Hammerman, the Pushcart King

At the time of the Pushcart War, Morris the Florist had been in the flower line for forty-three years. He was a soft-spoken man, and his only claim to fame before the war was that it was impossible to buy a dozen flowers from him.

If a customer asked Morris for a dozen tulips—or daffodils or mixed snapdragons—Morris always wrapped up thirteen flowers.

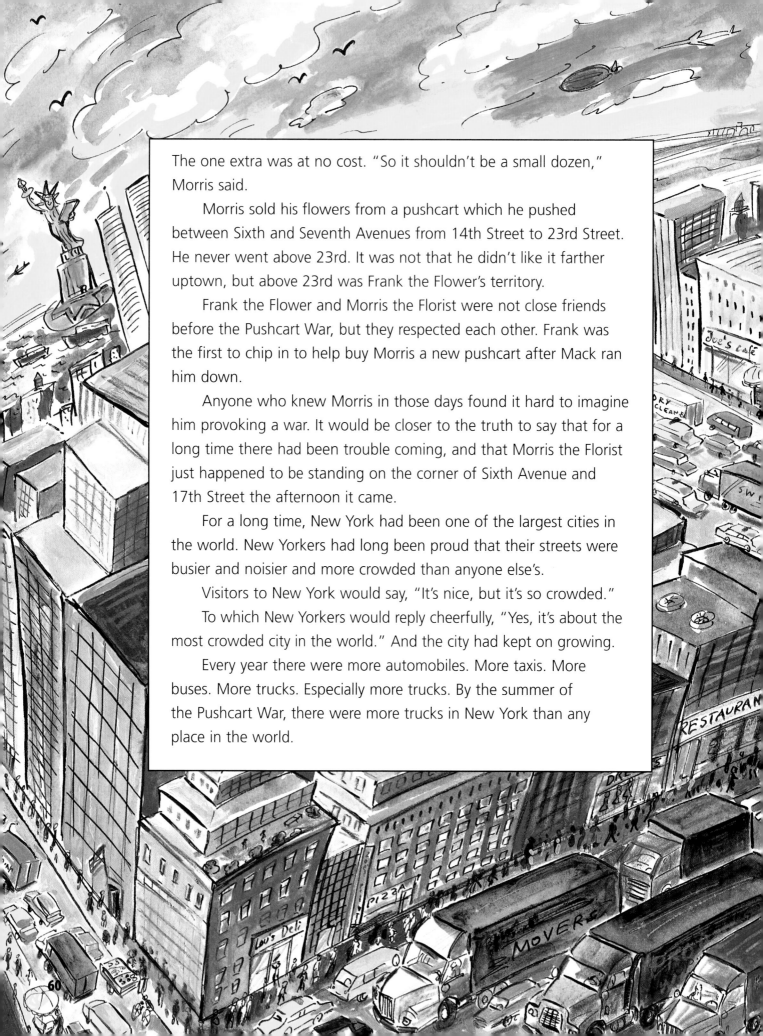

The one extra was at no cost. "So it shouldn't be a small dozen," Morris said.

Morris sold his flowers from a pushcart which he pushed between Sixth and Seventh Avenues from 14th Street to 23rd Street. He never went above 23rd. It was not that he didn't like it farther uptown, but above 23rd was Frank the Flower's territory.

Frank the Flower and Morris the Florist were not close friends before the Pushcart War, but they respected each other. Frank was the first to chip in to help buy Morris a new pushcart after Mack ran him down.

Anyone who knew Morris in those days found it hard to imagine him provoking a war. It would be closer to the truth to say that for a long time there had been trouble coming, and that Morris the Florist just happened to be standing on the corner of Sixth Avenue and 17th Street the afternoon it came.

For a long time, New York had been one of the largest cities in the world. New Yorkers had long been proud that their streets were busier and noisier and more crowded than anyone else's.

Visitors to New York would say, "It's nice, but it's so crowded."

To which New Yorkers would reply cheerfully, "Yes, it's about the most crowded city in the world." And the city had kept on growing.

Every year there were more automobiles. More taxis. More buses. More trucks. Especially more trucks. By the summer of the Pushcart War, there were more trucks in New York than any place in the world.

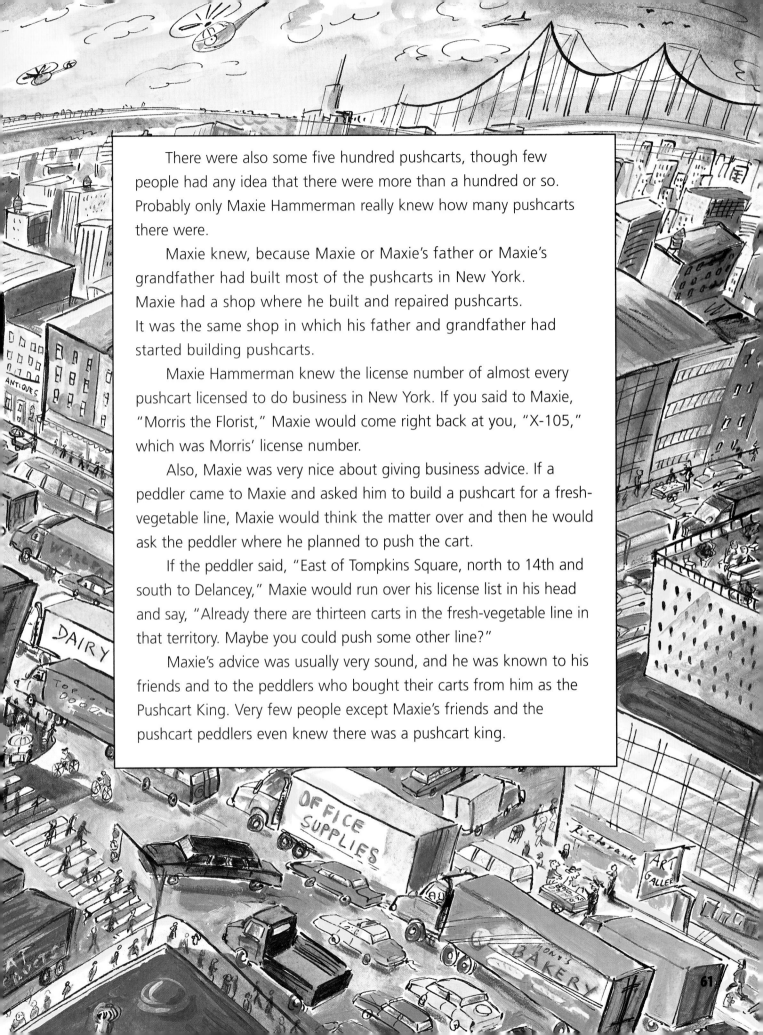

There were also some five hundred pushcarts, though few people had any idea that there were more than a hundred or so. Probably only Maxie Hammerman really knew how many pushcarts there were.

Maxie knew, because Maxie or Maxie's father or Maxie's grandfather had built most of the pushcarts in New York. Maxie had a shop where he built and repaired pushcarts. It was the same shop in which his father and grandfather had started building pushcarts.

Maxie Hammerman knew the license number of almost every pushcart licensed to do business in New York. If you said to Maxie, "Morris the Florist," Maxie would come right back at you, "X-105," which was Morris' license number.

Also, Maxie was very nice about giving business advice. If a peddler came to Maxie and asked him to build a pushcart for a fresh-vegetable line, Maxie would think the matter over and then he would ask the peddler where he planned to push the cart.

If the peddler said, "East of Tompkins Square, north to 14th and south to Delancey," Maxie would run over his license list in his head and say, "Already there are thirteen carts in the fresh-vegetable line in that territory. Maybe you could push some other line?"

Maxie's advice was usually very sound, and he was known to his friends and to the peddlers who bought their carts from him as the Pushcart King. Very few people except Maxie's friends and the pushcart peddlers even knew there was a pushcart king.

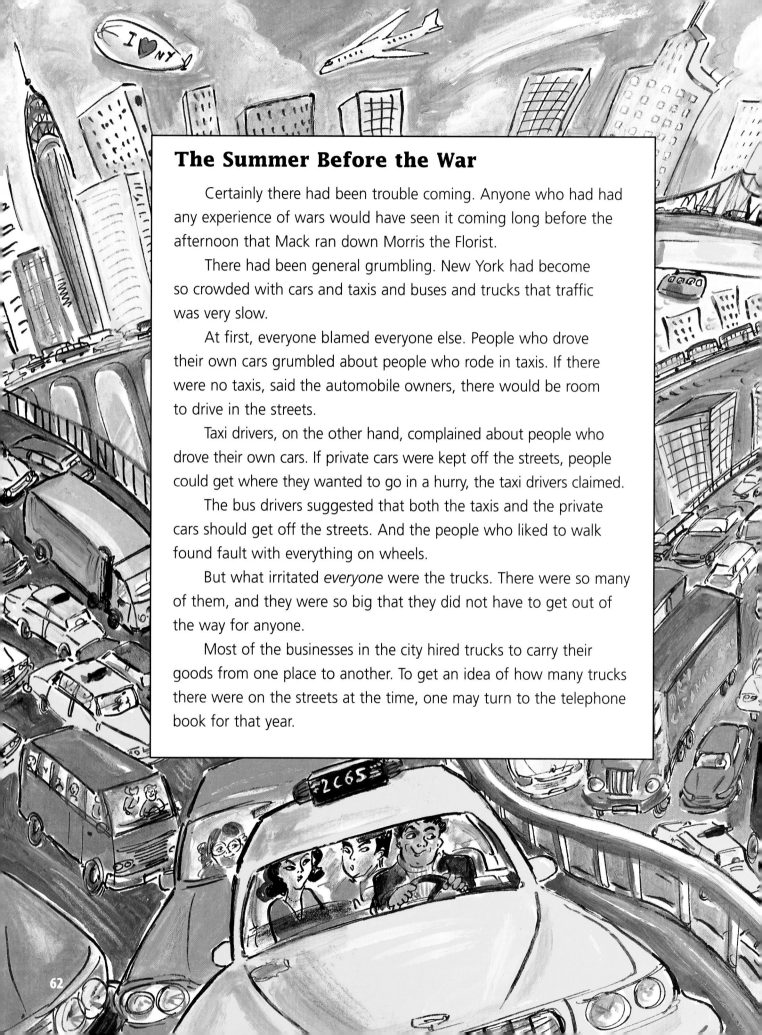

The Summer Before the War

Certainly there had been trouble coming. Anyone who had had any experience of wars would have seen it coming long before the afternoon that Mack ran down Morris the Florist.

There had been general grumbling. New York had become so crowded with cars and taxis and buses and trucks that traffic was very slow.

At first, everyone blamed everyone else. People who drove their own cars grumbled about people who rode in taxis. If there were no taxis, said the automobile owners, there would be room to drive in the streets.

Taxi drivers, on the other hand, complained about people who drove their own cars. If private cars were kept off the streets, people could get where they wanted to go in a hurry, the taxi drivers claimed.

The bus drivers suggested that both the taxis and the private cars should get off the streets. And the people who liked to walk found fault with everything on wheels.

But what irritated *everyone* were the trucks. There were so many of them, and they were so big that they did not have to get out of the way for anyone.

Most of the businesses in the city hired trucks to carry their goods from one place to another. To get an idea of how many trucks there were on the streets at the time, one may turn to the telephone book for that year.

In the classified section, for instance, if one opens to the "P" listings, a few of the products one will find advertised there are:

Package Handles
Paint
Pajama Trimmings
Pancake Mixes
Pants
Paper Plates
Parachutes
Park Benches
Parking Meters
Parquet Floors
Party Favors
Paste
Patent Medicines
Patterns
Paving Brick
Pawn Tickets
Peas
Peanut Butter
Pearls
Pecans
Pencils
Pen Knives
Penicillin
Pennants
Pens
Pepper
Perambulators
Percales
Perfumes
Periodicals
Permanent Wave Machines
Pet Shop Supplies
Petroleum
Pewter
Pharmaceuticals
Phonographs
Photographic Supplies
Piano Stools
Piccolos
Pickle Barrels
Picnic Tables

Picture Frames
Picture Post Cards
Picture Windows
Pies
Pigskins
Pile Drivers
Pillows
Pins
Pipe
Pipe Organs
Pistol Belts
Piston Rings
Pizza Pie Supplies
Place Cards
Planetariums
Plant Foods
Plaques
Plaster of Paris
Plastics
Plate Glass
Platforms
Platinum
Playground Equipment
Playing Cards
Playsuits
Playthings
Pleating Machine Part
Plexiglass
Pliers
Plows
Plugs
Plumbago
Plushes
Plywood
Pocketbooks
Podiums
Poker Chips
Poisons
Poles
Police Badges
Polish

Polo Mallets
Pompoms
Ponchos
Pony Carts
Pool Tables
Popcorn Machines
Porch Furniture
Postage Stamp Affixers
Posters
Potatoes
Potato Peelers
Pot Holders
Potted Plants
Pottery
Poultry
Powder Puffs
Precious Stones
Precision Castings
Premium Goods
Preserves
Pressing Machines
Pressure Cookers
Pretzels
Price Tags
Printing Presses
Propellers
Projectors
Prunes
Public Address Systems
Publications
Pulleys
Pulpits
Pumice
Pumps
Punch Bowls
Puppets
Purses
Pushcart Parts
Putty
Puzzles

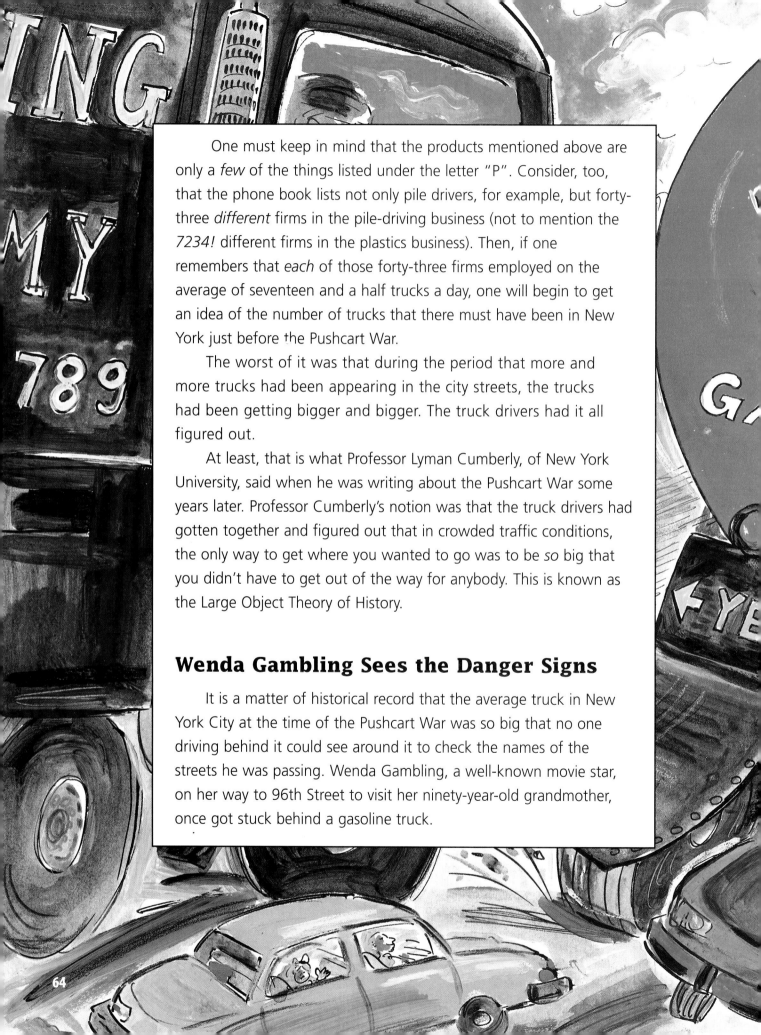

One must keep in mind that the products mentioned above are only a *few* of the things listed under the letter "P". Consider, too, that the phone book lists not only pile drivers, for example, but forty-three *different* firms in the pile-driving business (not to mention the *7234!* different firms in the plastics business). Then, if one remembers that *each* of those forty-three firms employed on the average of seventeen and a half trucks a day, one will begin to get an idea of the number of trucks that there must have been in New York just before the Pushcart War.

The worst of it was that during the period that more and more trucks had been appearing in the city streets, the trucks had been getting bigger and bigger. The truck drivers had it all figured out.

At least, that is what Professor Lyman Cumberly, of New York University, said when he was writing about the Pushcart War some years later. Professor Cumberly's notion was that the truck drivers had gotten together and figured out that in crowded traffic conditions, the only way to get where you wanted to go was to be *so* big that you didn't have to get out of the way for anybody. This is known as the Large Object Theory of History.

Wenda Gambling Sees the Danger Signs

It is a matter of historical record that the average truck in New York City at the time of the Pushcart War was so big that no one driving behind it could see around it to check the names of the streets he was passing. Wenda Gambling, a well-known movie star, on her way to 96th Street to visit her ninety-year-old grandmother, once got stuck behind a gasoline truck.

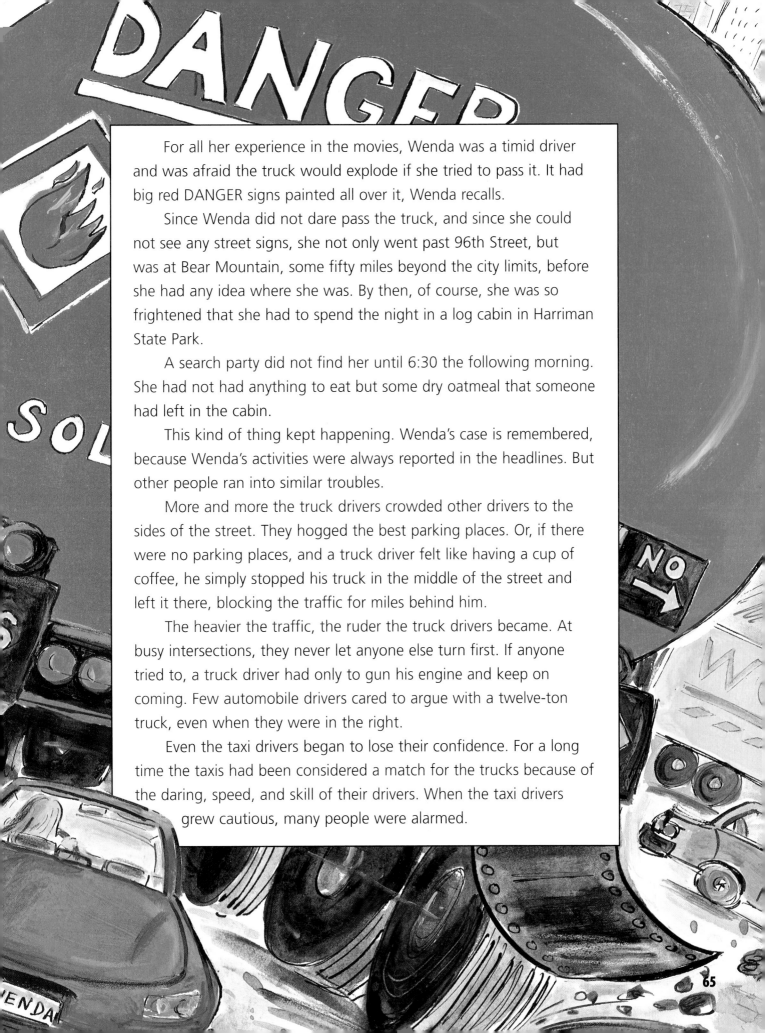

For all her experience in the movies, Wenda was a timid driver and was afraid the truck would explode if she tried to pass it. It had big red DANGER signs painted all over it, Wenda recalls.

Since Wenda did not dare pass the truck, and since she could not see any street signs, she not only went past 96th Street, but was at Bear Mountain, some fifty miles beyond the city limits, before she had any idea where she was. By then, of course, she was so frightened that she had to spend the night in a log cabin in Harriman State Park.

A search party did not find her until 6:30 the following morning. She had not had anything to eat but some dry oatmeal that someone had left in the cabin.

This kind of thing kept happening. Wenda's case is remembered, because Wenda's activities were always reported in the headlines. But other people ran into similar troubles.

More and more the truck drivers crowded other drivers to the sides of the street. They hogged the best parking places. Or, if there were no parking places, and a truck driver felt like having a cup of coffee, he simply stopped his truck in the middle of the street and left it there, blocking the traffic for miles behind him.

The heavier the traffic, the ruder the truck drivers became. At busy intersections, they never let anyone else turn first. If anyone tried to, a truck driver had only to gun his engine and keep on coming. Few automobile drivers cared to argue with a twelve-ton truck, even when they were in the right.

Even the taxi drivers began to lose their confidence. For a long time the taxis had been considered a match for the trucks because of the daring, speed, and skill of their drivers. When the taxi drivers grew cautious, many people were alarmed.

The Peanut Butter Speech

One of the first people to speak out against the growing danger was a man named Archie Love. Archie Love was running for Mayor at the time, and he promised to reduce the number of trucks in the streets.

It looked briefly as if Archie Love might be elected on the strength of this promise alone. But that was before Archie's opponent, Emmett P. Cudd (who was already Mayor and did not want to lose his job), made his famous "Peanut Butter Speech" in Union Square.

Mayor Cudd repeated the Peanut Butter Speech ninety times in one week. It went more or less as follows:

"Friends and New Yorkers: New York is one of the biggest cities in the U.S.A. We are proud of that fact.

"What makes a city big? Big business, naturally.

"And what is the difference between big business and small business? It is this: If you order fourteen cartons of peanut butter, you are running a small business. If you order four hundred cartons of peanut butter, you are running a big business.

"Fourteen cartons of peanut butter, you can get delivered in a station wagon. But for four hundred cartons of peanut butter, you need a truck. And you need a *big* truck. Big trucks mean progress.

"My opponent, Archie Love, is against trucks. He is, therefore, against progress. Maybe he is even against peanut butter."

Naturally, all the truck drivers voted to re-elect Mayor Cudd, and so did a lot of other people. Very few people wanted to be against progress. No one wanted to be against peanut butter. And *everyone* wanted to be proud of their city, because they always had been. Thus, Archie Love did not get elected, and the trucks kept getting bigger.

As the trucks increased in size, traffic—as Archie Love had predicted—grew steadily worse until, in the spring before the Pushcart War, the city was one big traffic jam most of the time. One day it took a taxi four hours to drive five blocks.

The passenger in the taxi was Professor Lyman Cumberly, who did not complain because he was working on his Large Object Theory of History and found the situation interesting from a scientific point of view. During this ride, Professor Cumberly fell into conversation with an impatient young man from Seattle who was trapped in an adjoining taxi.

The young man was shocked that so many New Yorkers accepted the terrible conditions in their streets without protest, and Professor Cumberly recalls that the visitor had very definite ideas what should be done about the trucks. In fact, encouraged by Professor Cumberly's interest, the young man flew back to Seattle and wrote a book.

The book, called *The Enemy in the Streets*, was a fearless attack on the trucks. However, as the author was unknown, the book did not receive much notice at the time it was published. It is remembered today largely because the author is now President of the United States.

The Words That Triggered the War (Wenda Gambling's Innocent Remark)

What finally brought matters to a head was a television program called "The Day the Traffic Stopped." The day before the program, the traffic *had* stopped entirely, and one of the television stations had hurriedly called in a panel of experts to explain why.

The members of the panel were:

Robert Alexander Wrightson—Traffic Commissioner of New York

Alexander P. Wolfson—head of Wolfson & Wolfson, specialists in traffic coordination

Dr. Wolfe Alexander—a traffic psychologist

Wenda Gambling—a well-known movie star

Wenda Gambling was hardly an expert on traffic. But as the three other panel members were elderly men (one stout, one bald, and one near-sighted), the moderator of the program felt that the panel would be more interesting to the audience if Wenda were at the table.

In introducing Wenda, the moderator of the program said, "As we all know, Miss Gambling's new movie, *The Streets of New York*, is being shot on the streets of New York, and as the streets of New York are the subject of our discussion tonight, it is very appropriate that she should be here."

Wenda tactfully left most of the talking to the experts. Each of the three men had a different theory as to why the traffic had stopped.

Robert Alexander Wrightson said that there was no cause for alarm, that the whole thing was a simple matter of what he liked to call "the density of moving objects."

Alexander P. Wolfson disagreed. He said the problem involved nothing more than "a predictable increase in the number of unmoving objects."

Dr. Wolfe Alexander said that it did not matter whether the objects were moving or unmoving as the whole thing could be easily solved by "a more thorough conditioning of drivers to hopeless situations."

"And what do you think, Miss Gambling?" asked the moderator, as the three experts began to argue with each other.

"I don't know what they are talking about," said Wenda Gambling.

"Well," said the moderator, who was not quite sure himself, "I believe our subject this evening was traffic."

"Oh," said Wenda Gambling. "Well, I think that there are too many trucks and that the trucks are too big."

Since most of the television audience had been watching Wenda Gambling rather than the experts—and since everyone watching *did* know what Wenda was talking about—this one remark received more attention than anything else that was said on the program. Before the program was off the air, over five thousand viewers had called the station to say that they agreed with Wenda Gambling.

Professor Lyman Cumberly has suggested that except for Wenda Gambling's innocent remark, there might never have been a Pushcart War. Instead, says Professor Cumberly, the trucks would have simply gone on taking over the city, crowding out the taxis, buses, cars—and finally the people themselves. No one would have challenged them until it was too late.

It would, Professor Cumberly believes, have been the end of life in New York as we know it. But once Wenda Gambling had stated the danger for all to hear, war was inevitable.

Karen Heit

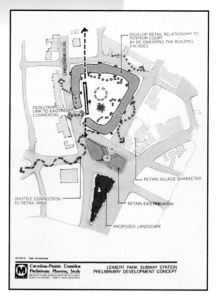

Crenshaw–Prairie Corridor
Preliminary Planning Study

LEIMERT PARK SUBWAY STATION
PRELIMINARY DEVELOPMENT CONCEPT

Urban Planner

Urban planners *plot* the future of our cities.

The job of any urban planner is to think of ways to improve a city's future. In Los Angeles a better transportation system is needed. Each day millions of cars jam the city's freeways and pollute its air. The residents of Los Angeles hope to see an improved traffic situation in their future. That's where Karen Heit comes in. She's an urban planner specializing in transportation.

PROFILE

Name: Karen Heit

Occupation: urban planner for the Los Angeles County Transportation Authority

Job title: Director, South Bay Area Team

Pets: two dogs, two turtles, a tadpole, and a tarantula

Favorite place to go in L.A.: the beach

Favorite way to get around L.A.: walking—until the subway system is completed!

Long Beach

UESTIONS
for Karen Heit

Here's how *urban planner* Karen Heit gets L.A. moving.

 What kind of transportation problems does Los Angeles have?

 For 20 years, L.A. has been known for having one of the worst traffic situations in the country. During an event like an L.A. Lakers basketball game, the highways become one big parking lot.

 So what's the solution?

 It lies in expanding the rail system. We've got two lines running now, but we need to build many more.

 How do you plan the rail lines?

 First, my staff and I determine the best place to run the lines. We conduct surveys and talk with community members to come up with possible locations.

 What happens next?

 I plot out routes for the lines on maps. It can take 12 to 13 years to complete a rail line! When the lines are up and

running, we continue to deal with the concerns of the people who live near them. We hold community meetings on a regular basis to get input from residents.

Q Will the rail lines help the community in other ways besides easing traffic?

A Absolutely. Our latest line will be built in a high-unemployment area. The line should attract new businesses and services, making the area a better place to live.

Q In your opinion, what quality helps an urban planner most?

A The number-one resource for urban planning is imagination. We have to be able to visualize a community springing back to life, then make it happen.

Karen Heit's
Tips for Assessing and Responding

1 Survey community residents to find out what sorts of improvements they would most like to see in their community.

2 Interview local business owners and service persons to learn about the commercial needs of the area.

3 Meet with community members to get their feedback about changes in the community.

From Garbage!

Where It Comes From, Where It Goes

AWARD WINNING

Book

by Evan and Janet Hadingham

Imagine walking in New York City on a hot summer day. Sweaty pedestrians packed on the pavements, taxi horns, police sirens, sticky air, and traffic fumes can all make your walk pretty unpleasant. But that's nothing compared to what it was like about a hundred years ago.

Back then, there were no regular city-wide collections of garbage. You tossed your trash in wooden barrels lined up on the pavement. In between the barrels were big piles of coal or wood ash on which you dumped the ashes from your fireplace each morning. And you probably didn't think twice about throwing food or even toilet waste directly into the gutter.

But when you ventured out for a walk, you could scarcely ignore the filthy streets of New York. If you were a woman, you were wearing long skirts and had to lift them frequently to avoid the messes on the sidewalk. On some street corners you could scarcely breathe because of the fumes from breweries, slaughterhouses, and factories, combined with the stink from the gutter.

◀

Putting out the garbage on Ludlow Street, New York City, in 1881. The sidewalks were littered with heaps of ashes emptied from fireplaces and furnaces.

▲

Since 1900, New York's garbage trucks have improved, but the job they do has stayed much the same. At a city waterfront, trucks tip trash onto barges in 1980 (top) and around 1900 (bottom).

WOW!

AMAZING GARBAGE FACT

Boxes, Boxes Everywhere

In just one day, Americans toss out 150,000 tons (136,000 metric tons) of packaging material. This amount would fill about 10,000 tractor trailers. If all the trucks were lined up end-to-end, they would stretch for 120 miles (190 km).

Get Nosey About Your Garbage

Be a garbage detective. Figure out what goes into your garbage pail: Is it mostly food scraps or packaging? Do some research. For one week, instead of tossing packaging material into your regular garbage pail, collect it in a separate cardboard box.

Then try to identify the different materials (plastic, paper, aluminum, etc.). Notice the many different types of plastic— some are stiff, others light and supple; can you tell why that particular type of plastic was chosen for each package?

Can you figure out the main purpose of each packaging item? Was it to keep the food fresh? To protect it from damage during shipping? Do you think any of the items are examples of *overpackaging*— packaging that's there simply to make the item bigger and more eye-catching?

Continue your detective work next time you're at the grocery store. Which are the most overpackaged brands? If you or your parents avoid buying them, you'll be helping to solve the garbage problem.

And even though today's car fumes can make New York unpleasant and unhealthy, "exhaust" from horses presented quite a problem in the days before the automobile. A century ago, Brooklyn's horses produced 200 tons (180 metric tons) of manure a day (enough to fill eight railroad freight cars). In springtime, farmers visited the city with wagons and removed some of the horse manure to spread on their fields as fertilizer. But by summer, much of it ended up ground into the mud in the city's unpaved back alleys.

Many of New York's poor neighborhoods were so filthy and overcrowded that serious diseases such as typhoid and cholera spread easily. One such outbreak in 1892 helped shake up citizens and officials, who finally realized that garbage had become a serious problem. But how could they solve it?

The first solution was to dump it at sea. Around 1900, most of New York's trash was loaded on barges, towed out of the harbor for about ten miles (16 km), then heaved into the Atlantic. Bathers at New Jersey's crowded beaches were sometimes startled when they swam up against objects such as floating mattresses and dead dogs. In fact, the problem became so bad that New Jersey's state officials forced New York City to stop ocean dumping in 1933.

But even today, many east coast beaches are forced to close down for days or weeks during the summer. The reason? Washed-up trash, sewage, sometimes even waste from hospitals that may carry germs or viruses. Some of the garbage is spilled accidentally or blown from landfills close to the ocean, like New York's giant trash mound at Fresh Kills on Staten Island. But much of it is dumped illegally. While New York and other coastal cities were forced to give up ocean dumping long ago, the pollution continues.

Some people with a garbage problem on their hands are still prepared to break the law and use the ocean as a dump.

▶
Around 1900, most of New York City's trash was carried out to the harbor in barges, where it was shoveled into the sea.

▶
Trash dumped in New York's harbor would often drift down to New Jersey beaches to surprise bathers.

A Day in the Life of New York's Garbage

Every day, 1,000 garbage trucks crawl through the streets of New York City, each operated by a two-person crew. After picking up a full load, the crew drives its truck to one of thirteen different piers on the city's waterfront. There they put the truck into reverse and back it up to the edge of the pier, dumping their load into a barge waiting in the water below. Each

Today, New York's eight million residents throw out enough garbage every month to fill up the Empire State Building. After curbside collection, most of it ends up on barges that are towed past the skyscrapers of Manhattan and out into the harbor.

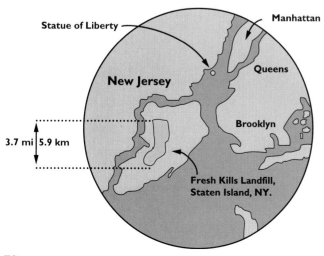

Statue of Liberty
Manhattan
New Jersey
Queens
Brooklyn
3.7 mi 5.9 km
Fresh Kills Landfill, Staten Island, NY.

barge can hold 6,000 tons of trash. Tugboats then pull the barges across the harbor to their destination: the world's largest dump, Fresh Kills, on Staten Island. ("Kills" comes from the original Dutch settlers' word for "channel.") This dump covers an area of 3,000 acres (1,215 ha), equal to 16,000 baseball diamonds.

Once the barges arrive, giant cranes shift the trash into wagons, which are then pulled by tractors up onto the summit of Fresh Kills. Bulldozers help spread the trash and cover it with dirt. In summer, water containing insecticide is sprayed everywhere to keep down the clouds of dust and flies.

After ocean dumping was banned in 1933, New York's garbage had nowhere to go except to dumps like Fresh Kills and to a few *incinerators* (garbage-burning plants). For a while, dump sites were plentiful. But as the city grew and more and more New Yorkers objected to living near the dumps, one by one they were shut down.

The barges finally arrive at Fresh Kills on Staten Island, where a giant crane unloads the trash and bulldozers push it around, creating a human-made mountain.

Fresh Kills is now one of only two dumps remaining in operation. The vast majority of the city's rubbish ends up here—some 22,000 tons (20,000 metric tons) of it a day. By the year 2000 or even earlier, Fresh Kills will be full and the city will have to come up with another garbage solution. By that time, the mound will be over five hundred feet (150m) high—about the height of the Washington Monument. It will be the highest spot on the eastern seaboard south of Maine.

The Packaging Explosion

Back when your great-grandparents were children, a trip to a grocery store was very different from what it is today. There was much less packaging and instead of picking up new bags from the store, you always took your own basket or canvas bag for carrying groceries home.

Many items were stored out of reach behind the counter. If you had a large family you probably bought big bags of flour and sugar. (And when the cotton sacks were empty, you didn't throw them away. Instead, you bleached and sewed them into children's underwear.)

Every Day Americans Throw Out:

an average of about 4 pounds (1.8 kg) of garbage each. If you piled everyone's daily trash together in a single giant heap, it would weigh more than 438,000 tons (398,000 metric tons). Or if you managed to load it all into garbage trucks, you would need 63,000 of them. Lined up end to end, these 63,000 trucks would stretch for nearly 370 miles (600 km), about the distance from San Francisco to Los Angeles.

A few food items were sold in metal cans, but these were expensive. Besides, like most people, you probably did your own canning in glass jars that you used again year after year. If you did buy canned food, you kept the cans to store household objects like nails or buttons.

In 1879, a businessman named Frank Woolworth opened the first five-and-ten store in upstate New York. (It was called five-and-ten because back then many items cost a dime or less.) Woolworth was the first to pioneer the idea of displaying store goods on open shelves so that customers could see and touch the items themselves.

In the Days Before Plastic

Ask the oldest person you know what it was like to go shopping when he or she was a child. Were there grocery carts? How many kinds of breakfast cereal were available? What came in cans? How were groceries brought home from the store? Was any packaging material saved and reused? What happened to food scraps? How was life different without the convenience foods we have today?

This meant there had to be a lot more packaging of individual items, partly to catch the customer's eye and partly to make it a little harder for anyone to slip the items into a pocket and steal them from the store.

Packaging also keeps food fresh longer, and that helped to make the whole idea of convenience foods possible. But the popularity of such items as ready-made soups, cake mixes, and frozen dinners has led to an explosion in the amount of disposable plastic, paper, and aluminum we take into our homes at the end of every shopping trip.

So many items crowd the supermarket shelves that food companies compete with each other to make their packages brighter, shinier, more appealing. That means a lot of overpackaging—far more than is necessary to keep food from spoiling. And it costs us all money: One out of every ten dollars you spend on groceries pays for the cost of packaging them.

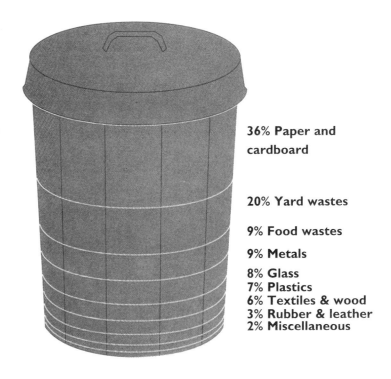

What's in our trash: This diagram gives a rough idea of the different percentages of materials typically thrown out by Americans.

36% Paper and cardboard

20% Yard wastes

9% Food wastes

9% Metals

8% Glass
7% Plastics
6% Textiles & wood
3% Rubber & leather
2% Miscellaneous

Throwaway World

In 1955, *Life* magazine reported on a popular trend—"throwaway living." The 1950s were a boom time for middle-class Americans. They had been through years of restrictions and shortages during the Second World War, when they had to save every little scrap. Now they rushed out to buy disposable plates, knives, forks, frying pans, diapers—anything that promised to cut down on tedious chores. In this article, *Life* also reported on bizarre items such as disposable curtains, disposable duck-hunting decoys, and a 79-cent barbeque grill that you used once and tossed out.

While many items never caught on, a lot of products today are still designed to be used only once or twice. For instance, think of plastic shaving razors, mini-

Throwaway Living in the 1990s

Each year, Americans get rid of 350 million disposable plastic cigarette lighters, 1½ billion ballpoint pens, and 2 billion plastic shaving razors.

flashlights that you throw out once the bulb burns out, disposable cameras good for only one roll of film...all bound for the garbage, sooner rather than later.

Some brands of VCRs, hair dryers, telephones, and other appliances are built so cheaply that they only last a year or two. When they break, it often costs less to buy a new one than to have the old one repaired. And so it ends up in the trash, too.

SOURCE

Ranger Rick

Magazine

50
CAN-DO
KIDS

By Kathy Love

Photos by
Paul Childress

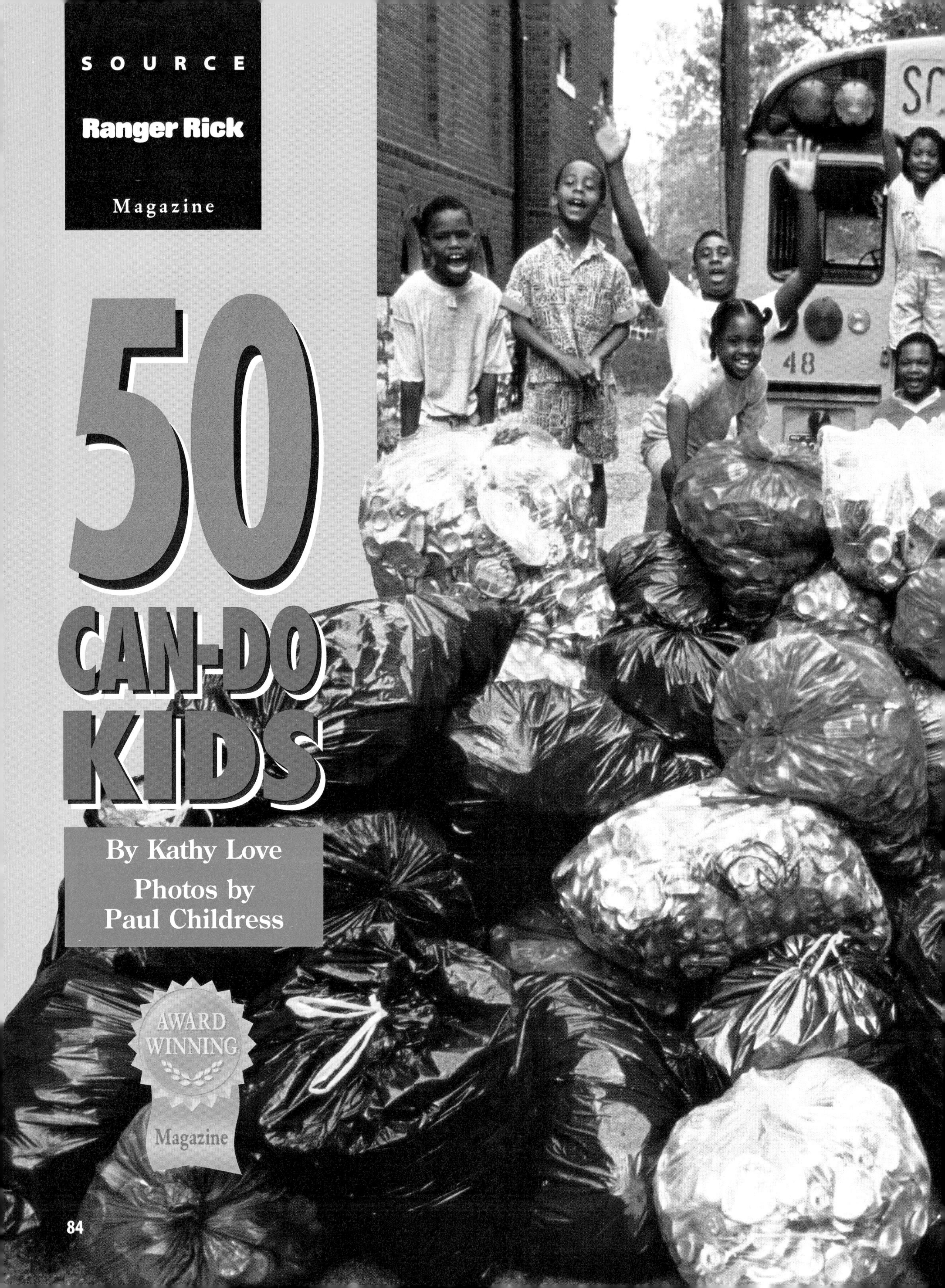

AWARD
WINNING

Magazine

In 1987, a man named Neil Andre decided to start a new environmental group. "Great!" his friends said. Then he told them he was going to start it with inner-city kids (kids who live in the poorest part of the city). "You're crazy!" they told him.

"Everyone said that kids can't do anything about the environment," Neil remembers, "and that inner-city kids have too many other problems to worry about besides the Earth."

Oh, yeah?

Meet the Dolphin Defenders—a church group of 50 kids in fifth and sixth grade from St. Louis, Missouri. (We'll tell you later why they're called Dolphin Defenders.) Since this group got started, they've won 60 national awards for their work for the environment.

The Dolphin Defenders pile up 48,000 aluminum cans they collected on their city streets.

Think Globally, Act Locally

The kids raise money for environmental projects in the United States and around the world. But mostly, the Defenders work for the environment close to home. They've helped their neighbor-hood in lots of ways:

- *The kids hold Trash Bashes, Glass Passes, and Can Scans to clean up their neighborhood.*

- *They hunt through dumpsters for good junk. Then they reuse the items by turning them into things such as furniture or game pieces. Or they sell them to raise money.*

- *The Defenders have recycled 15,000 pounds (6750 kg) of glass and over 193,000 aluminum cans. Now they've started recycling used tires.*

- *They've created four wildlife habitats under a program run by the National Wildlife Federation (the group that publishes* Ranger Rick*). The habitats are now home to many plants and animals. "We have bird feeders and birdbaths in our wildlife habitats, where we can watch cardinals, chickadees, blue jays—lots of different birds," says Dolphin Defender Lela Ford. The areas have even attracted raccoons, opossums, and a red fox family!*

Number One Problem: Drugs

For the Defenders, cleaning up their city neighborhood is no easy thing. Gangs and drug dealers roam through the area, taking over the local park and some of the streets. The kids have learned to clean up the park in the morning. That way, they're out of there before the drug dealers arrive in the afternoon.

The Defenders try to teach their neighbors about the environment. For example, they talked to local people about a plan to turn part of a city park into a parking lot. The people then voted to save the park.

The Defenders also ask people not to litter. But it doesn't always

Dolphin Defenders are totally into trash bashing. They roam the streets looking for stuff to recycle (left).

work. "Some people don't care about cleaning up the environment," says Defender Dianna Hogan. "They just want to drive around in big cars, play loud music, and throw their trash everywhere. If you tell them not to, they get mad."

Some people do worse things than litter. The Defenders spent 85 hard-earned dollars to buy a top-of-the-line bird feeder for one of their habitats. But some people from the neighborhood destroyed it.

"The Defenders live with violence every day," says their leader. "Some of them have had family members killed by gangs. But the amazing thing about them is that they're able to look beyond their own problems and focus on the problems of planet Earth."

So why do they work for the environment? The Defenders say it makes them feel good. "If you really like what you're doing, it doesn't seem like work," says Dianna Hogan.

Neil thinks another reason is that the kids

believe they need to defend the Earth. Their belief shows in their name —Dolphin Defenders.

When dolphins are attacked, Neil says, they cooperate with each other to defend against the attack. "So the kids try to defend the Earth the same way dolphins defend each other," Neil explains. "That's why they call themselves the Dolphin Defenders."

Defending the Earth turns out to be something these kids are really good at. "See?" says Neil. "An environmental group with inner-city kids *wasn't* such a crazy idea!"

How to
Write a Needs Assessment

Nobody knows the needs of a community or neighborhood better than the people who live and work there. Before any changes or improvements are made in the community, its residents and businesspeople should be consulted. Conducting a needs assessment is one way to find out what community members think.

What is a needs assessment? Often, a needs assessment takes the form of a survey. People who write a needs-assessment survey have identified a problem they want to solve or an area they want to improve. The survey takers turn to community members to find out whether they agree.

An introduction tells the purpose of the survey.

Questions in surveys are numbered. Space is provided for the person's answers.

Rating systems allow the respondents to tell what's most important to them.

Questions that have a quick yes or no answer help determine whether people agree.

CORNERSTONE POOL

CUSTOMER
SATISFACTION
SURVEY

Cornerstone Pool is an aquatics pool facility located at 55 Buena Vista Road in West Hartford. The town is considering making changes and improvements to Cornerstone Pool. We are conducting a survey of the people who use Cornerstone to see how you feel about the facility and what changes you would want to see at the facility. Your input is important! When you turn in a completed survey, you will be given a free guest pass to Cornerstone. This is our way of saying thanks for taking the time to complete the survey.

1. How many visits a month on the average do you make to Cornerstone Pool?_____

2. Please rank in order of importance (1, 2, 3) the 3 reasons you swim at Cornerstone Pool.

_____ Price is reasonable

_____ Convenient location

_____ Like the programs offered

_____ Other (please specify) _____

3. Please rank in order of frequency (1, 2, 3) the three programs you participate in most:

_____ Early Bird swim

_____ 11 AM - 1 PM adult swim

_____ 8 - 9 lap swim

_____ Youth instructional lessons

_____ Adult instructional lessons

_____ Weekend lap swim

4. Do you find the pool staff members to be friendly and courteous?

☐ Yes   ☐ No   ☐ Varies

5. Overall, do you feel that the pool itself is:

Clean	☐ Yes	☐ No
Safe	☐ Yes	☐ No
In good condition	☐ Yes	☐ No
Overcrowded	☐ Yes	☐ No

6. What are the three things you like most about Cornerstone?

_____

7. What are the three things you like least about Cornerstone?

_____

Open-ended questions require longer answers in order to get detailed ideas and input.

1 Choose a Topic

What should your survey be about? Start by brainstorming things that you think your community needs. Perhaps your community needs more movie theaters, better bike paths, a larger library or a public swimming pool.

TOOLS

- paper and pencil

Choose something from your list that interests you and that you know something about. Use a needs assessment survey to find out whether others feel the same way.

2 Plan Your Survey

Start by making a list of issues that your survey should cover. For example, if you think your community needs better bike paths, your survey should be designed to find out whether better bike paths really are a concern of people who live there. You might ask if people own bicycles, how often they ride, and their opinions about the safety of the road. Review your list to make sure you have covered all the issues that are important for your topic.

3 Write Your Survey

Once you've decided what to cover in your survey, you need to write questions. Decide which type of question is best for each issue you want to cover. Some issues can be covered by simple yes-or-no questions. Sometimes people find it easier to answer questions if you supply them with a number of answers to choose from. Open-ended questions let people give thorough answers. Try to write at least six questions. When you are finished, think of a title for your needs assessment survey. Make sure that the questions are easy to read and that there is enough space for people to answer them.

Tip As you review the completed surveys, record all the answers on one blank survey. Then add up the results.

4 Take Your Survey

Make at least ten copies of your survey. Decide to whom you will distribute it. Think about people who might care about your issue. Your friends or neighbors might be good choices. After you've collected your surveys, look at how people answered them. How many people are satisfied with the way things are? How many want to change things? What did most people want to change? Tally the results of your surveys and report your results to your class.

If You Are Using a Computer...

Type your survey on a computer so your form will be neat and easy for people to read.

THINK

How did your survey change or reinforce your ideas about what your community needs?

Karen Heit
Urban Planner ▶

City dwellers can work together to improve their quality of life.

Reaching Out

Find out how two make-believe gangs try to settle their differences. Meet real-life kids who work together to make their city beautiful.

Read a story about a homeless boy called Maniac Magee, who finds a special place with a new family.

PROJECT

Create an action plan to improve your community.

93

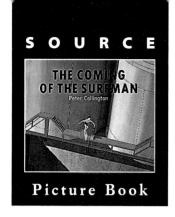
THE COMING OF THE SURFMAN

BY
Peter Collington

There are two gangs in my neighborhood: the Hammers and the Nails. They are sworn enemies.

I was skateboarding home one day when the Hammer gang grabbed me. Their leader, Hammerhead, lifted me off the ground by my collar, pushed his face close to mine, and showed me his fist.

"You're joining us," he said. It wasn't an invitation. It was a statement of fact. As I might want to smile again sometime—and it would be essential I had some teeth to do it with—I nodded.

"A wise decision," Hammerhead said, putting me down. "Now wear this." He handed me a red bandanna, the Hammers' color. As I walked away, struggling to put it around my head, I noticed the Nail gang up ahead. I quickly stuffed the bandanna into my pocket. Nailhead, the gang leader, looked me over. My foot tapped nervously on my skateboard. Nailhead's eyes lowered to my board.

"You wanna grow up. Skateboards are for kids." As I *was* a kid, it was quite logical that I should have a skateboard, but something made me keep quiet. It was my teeth again. Nailhead handed me a blue bandanna. "Wear this," he said. "You're one of us."

So I belong to two gangs, and if either of them finds out, I'm done for.

That night, I was lying awake thinking about my predicament when I heard a motor running. I looked out of my bedroom window and saw a van parked opposite, outside the boarded-up store. A man wearing beachwear stepped out. He looked around, the streetlight flashing on his sunglasses, and walked over to the store's front door. He jiggled with some keys and went in. He began unloading long cardboard cartons from his van.

After a while, I must have dropped off to sleep, but I was woken by the sound of an electric sander moaning and whining. The man had taken down the boards from the store window and was now working on the peeling paint.

The old store had closed down long ago because the owner was fed up with vandals breaking his windows and with neighborhood gangs harassing his customers. So a new store would be welcome.

The man had now opened some paint cans and was brightening up the woodwork. I couldn't wait until morning to find out what kind of a store it was going to be. A pizza place, a video rental shop—even a new food store would be fine. We wouldn't have to lug groceries from eight blocks away anymore.

Then my heart sank. I remembered the gangs and what they might do to me tomorrow.

When I got up and went outside, the two gangs were waiting for me. At least that's what I thought at first, but then I noticed they weren't looking at me but at the new store. The gangs stood well apart and were pointing to the window display.

Both Hammerhead and Nailhead took turns laughing and their respective gangs imitated them. The name of the store, emblazoned in bright neon lights, was SURFING SUPPLIES. In the store window were surfboards and different types of surfing wear.

I began to laugh myself, partly out of relief that the gangs had forgotten about me and partly because I shared their amusement. It was quite simple. There was nowhere around here to surf. The beach was a two-day drive away.

Who would open a store selling surfing stuff in a run-down neighborhood like this? Only someone who was two bread rolls short of a picnic. Someone who was seriously weird. The gangs laughed, and I laughed with them.

The SURFING SUPPLIES store opened regularly at nine o'clock every morning and closed at five-thirty on the dot. No one went into the store to buy anything, and no one came out.

The store owner became known as the Surfman, and people hooted and laughed whenever his name was mentioned. I didn't know what to think, but I was glad about one thing. Since he had come, the Hammers and Nails had forgotten entirely about me and hardly fought each other anymore. The blank, angry stares were gone; expression was leaking into their faces. I had seen that look before — especially in cats. It was a look of obsessive curiosity. Their brains were straining to figure out why the Surfman was here. Anyone weird could also be dangerous. So both gangs set up around-the-clock surveillance.

A pattern of behavior was emerging. Every Monday morning the Surfman cleaned his windows and swept the sidewalk. Once a month he took stock, even though he had sold nothing.

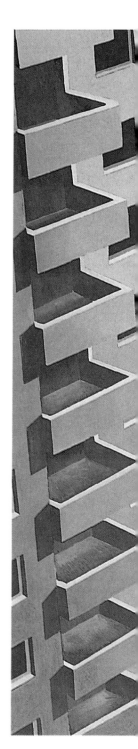

High-intensity binoculars revealed that he ate a mixed salad and yogurt for lunch and ran 200 miles a week on his exercise machine. He *had* to be training for something—but what?

Then one night I spotted him. He came out of his store about eleven o'clock and walked over to the abandoned factory across the way. He took out a large piece of paper and studied it by flashlight. He looked up at the factory and then down at the sheet of paper. He walked around the factory for a while and then went back to the store.

After this, the Surfman started appearing regularly at night, carrying a tool kit. He had more in common with the gangs than I had at first thought: he was very good at wrecking things. He was systematically demolishing the factory. It was crazy. Each night there was hammering and banging for hours on end. But as the weeks went by, there seemed to be some method in his madness.

With the help of the old factory crane, the Surfman ripped off the factory roof and sent the metal sheets crashing down onto the floor below. Then he began bolting the sheets onto the inner walls and floor. His long shadow spilled out over the ground as the light from his welding equipment flickered and darted. The Surfman rolled large pipes from the back of the factory and collected them together by the pump. Then he started bolting them together.

At the end of his night shift, he would stagger home, tired and drained, but he always opened the store, regular as clockwork, at nine o'clock, even though no one had ever seen a customer go in.

I began to really feel for him. He reminded me of my late dad, always working hard and no one giving him any thanks.

One evening, the Surfman erected scaffolding in front of
the two giant storage tanks and, with cutting equipment, began
burning into the metal. Every night something new was added or
changed, and in the light of day the two gangs would check out
the Surfman's progress. Occasionally, the gangs would take turns
flexing their muscles and knocking something down. But their
hearts weren't really in it, and when the Surfman repaired the
damage, they just shrugged and let things stand.

They, like me, wanted to see the Surfman complete his work. We
were all enthralled. We were trembling with anticipation. We all knew
what the Surfman was building, but nobody put it into words. The
Surfman jokes had died away, and a certain grudging respect was
apparent. He might be a weird guy, but he was a weird guy who was
making something for us. Something we had wanted all our lives.

One night, I was woken by the sound of running water. The
Surfman was standing by the metal pipes turning a large wheel
tap. He was wearing swimwear. As he pressed a switch, the pump
started throbbing and vibrating. The Surfman picked up his
surfboard and climbed high up the metal ladder to a position
overlooking the empty factory below. He leaned forward and
pulled a lever. The doors of the two storage tanks sprang open, and
WATER gushed out with all the ferocity of a giant surfing wave! The
Surfman was swept from his perch, only to reappear with his
surfboard under his feet and his arms stretched out on either side.
The Surfman was surfing! He rode the wave all the way to the end
of the factory, was carried up the metal slope, and then plummeted
ski-slope-style onto the piled-up car tires below.

The Surfman retrieved his surfboard and clambered down the tires. With his surfboard under his arm, he walked over to his store and went in. The wave machine wheezed and coughed, then spluttered to a halt. I always knew what it was going to be, but now I screamed the words out loud: "It's a WAVE MACHINE!" My voice echoed out of the window and ricocheted around the neighborhood. I heard whoops and cries of joy from Hammerhead and Nailhead, who had witnessed it too.

Tomorrow was going to be a great day.

In the morning, the two gangs were there early, clutching bits of wood and anything else they thought might do for a surfboard. When the wave machine started up, the gangs clambered up the ladder and, mixing together like one happy family, launched themselves and their bits of wood onto the wave. I just stood and watched. This was going to be fun. None of them had the slightest idea of how to surf, so they sank with their bits of wood and came up with furious faces, spurting water.

I had been saving up money for some time, not quite sure what to do with it. Now, I *knew!* As my dad used to say, "To do the job right, you need the right tool."

I walked over to the SURFING SUPPLIES store and put down my money. The Surfman handed me a real beauty of a board. He wasn't a talkative sort of guy. But as I left, he turned and said, "Have a good day."

I walked over to the wave machine and climbed up the stairs. The gangs stood back to watch. I waited until I heard the crash of water, and as the wave came, I stepped off. All the skateboarding had been good training. I held my balance and rode the crest of the wave for all it was worth. It was the best day of my life. The gangs tried to follow my example, but they had no balance, and their boards were rubbish. They knew what they had to do.

Nailhead led his gang in first. They all bought surfboards and walked proudly out of the Surfman's store. Next, Hammerhead led his gang into the store. When the Hammers came out, Nailhead was there to confront them. He swallowed hard. The words did not come easy to him.

"You wanna have a truce?" he asked.

Hammerhead looked back at his gang. They all nodded their heads. "Okay," said Hammerhead. "We surf alternate days." He held out his hand to shake.

"Done," said Nailhead.

The two gangs beamed at each other.

Nailhead took out a coin. "Heads or tails?"

Nailhead and his gang won the toss, and cheering, they ran over to the wave machine to try out their boards.

I put on my blue bandanna and joined them. The next day, I put on my red bandanna and joined the Hammers.

After a week, they found me out. I was thrown out of both gangs, and my surfing days were over. All I could do now was watch. I felt bored and depressed. Without surfing, life felt almost not worth living.

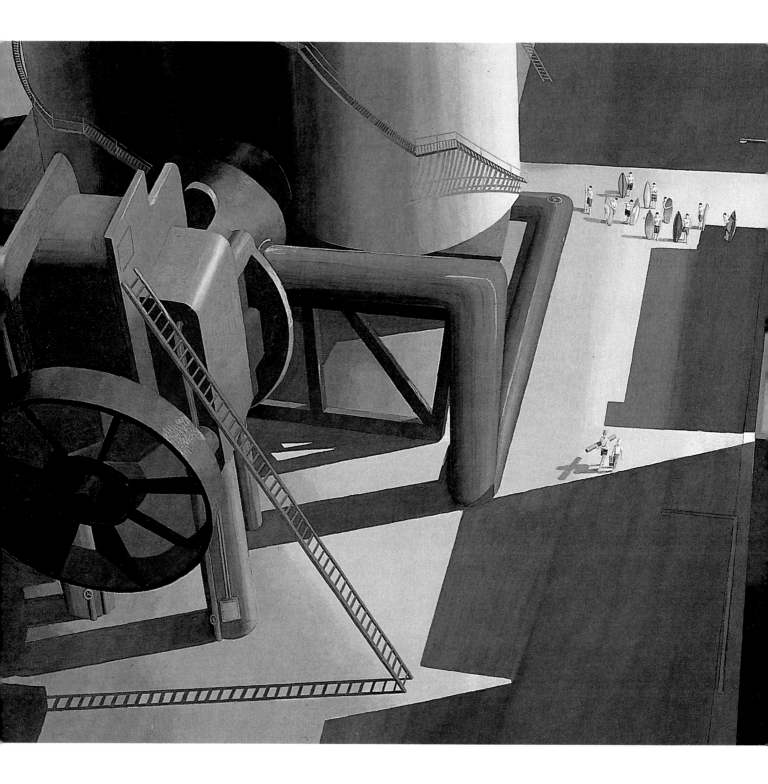

One day, I was enviously watching one of the gangs surfing when the pump suddenly ground to a halt. A cry of pain went up from every gang member's throat. The wave machine had broken down.

That evening, the Surfman came out of his shop and called me over. He handed me his tool kit, and I walked behind him over to the wave machine. I handed him each tool as he requested it, and when the job was finished, he turned to me and said, "Okay, try it out." I ran home and got my surfboard. I couldn't believe my luck. I tried one wave, curling down its crest and zigzagging in front of it.

"How is it?" called Surfman.

"Almost right," I answered. "I'll just check it out again." And this way I got to surf a second time—a long time—until I felt I was stretching the Surfman's patience and finally called out, "Yeah, it's fine now!" And the Surfman closed it down until the next day.

Fortunately, the wave machine broke down quite regularly, and I was always on hand to carry the Surfman's tool kit. As he worked, he talked to me, explaining what he was doing and why. He named each tool I handed to him as if he wanted me to remember what it was for the next time. The Surfman really did remind me of my late dad: *he* always liked to have me stand by him when he was fixing things. But I did the same thing now that I used to do with my dad. I humored him. I nodded and said "Yeah" a few times as if I were paying attention. But my mind wasn't there. It was focused on surfing and silently crying out for that moment when the Surfman would turn to me and say, "Okay, it's fixed. Go try it out." Then life for me would begin. Floating on those short-lived waves was everything to me.

On their enforced day of rest, while one gang surfed, the other spent its time jogging to the health food store in the next neighborhood for more supplies or sitting around watching surfing movies they had rented from the Surfman's store, analyzing and discussing good moves.

Then the truce broke down. The wave machine had been out of action for a whole day, so the Hammers felt they should surf the next day. The Nails insisted it was their turn, and fighting broke out. The Hammers, anticipating trouble, had come prepared. They had hidden their own surfboards, and producing axes and sledgehammers, they rushed over to the Nails' surfboards and began smashing them.

The result was catastrophic. The Nails let out agonizing screams of pain and doubled over on the ground, hugging the remains of their surfboards. They clutched them like babies and went home broken-hearted to try and fix them. The Hammers felt powerful—they had never been happier. They surfed all that day, confident that they would be surfing every day from now on.

But somehow I knew that would not be the end of it.

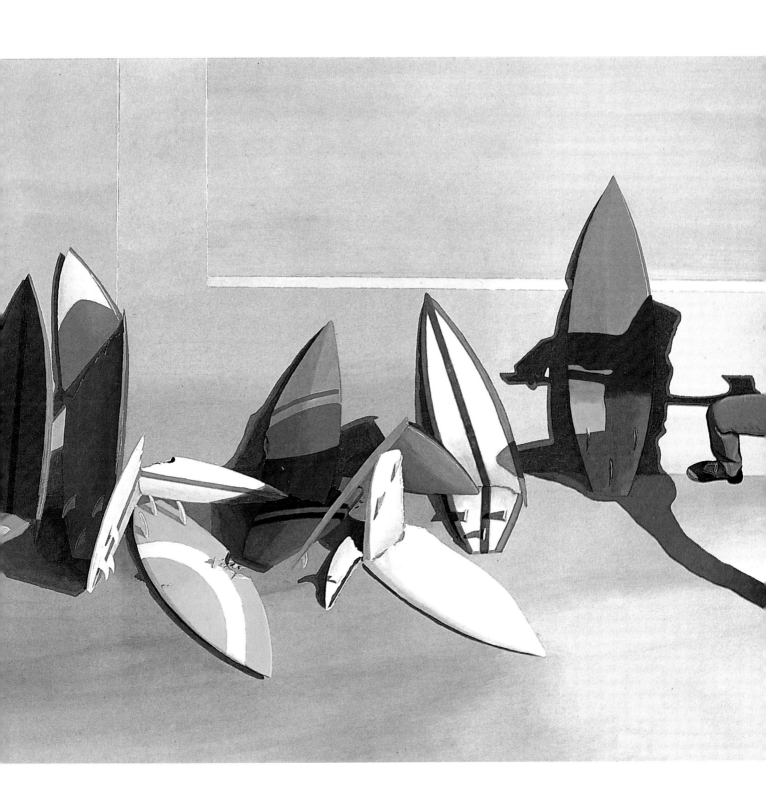

That night, I was woken by the sound of banging and crashing. Looking out of my bedroom window, I saw the Nail gang wielding axes and sledgehammers. They were smashing the wave machine. I quickly dressed and ran out to try and stop them. But it was too late. The Hammer gang was there too, and a big battle was taking place. I shouted and tried to reason with them, but no one took any notice of me. Water was spurting out of the pipes, and sparks were flying everywhere.

The following day, the two battle-weary and dejected gangs stood in front of the wave machine and looked at the damage they had caused. Their eyes looked over toward the Surfman's store. He had fixed things before. Surely he would fix things again.

Later that evening, I watched the Surfman walk out of his store and across to the battered wave machine. He stood for some time, just shaking his head. Then he walked home and into his store.

The next morning the Surfman had gone. His store was empty and the wave machine unrepaired. The two gangs stood in silence. Big tears rolled down their faces.

I ran back home to get my late dad's tool kit. The two gangs stepped aside to let me work. I tried various tools, pulling this way and that. But I knew in my heart it was hopeless. I couldn't remember what the Surfman had told me. I hadn't been listening. The gangs' hopeful eyes narrowed.

"Stupid kid," they said and walked away.

Things have gone pretty much back to normal here, the gangs once again fighting each other. Neither of them is interested in my joining them now, which is fine with me.

On bad days, I think about my father a lot and all the things I could have done with him if he were still alive. On good days, I feel sure that the Surfman will return, and this time I know I'll be ready and really listen to what he says and really watch his big hands as he works away at the rusting hulk of the wave machine, restoring it to good working order.

SOURCE

Newspaper

From the *Philadelphia Daily News*

AWARD WINNING

Newspaper

Art Show Draws Upon Ex-Graffiti Scrawlers

By Joseph P. Blake

THERE SEEMS TO be a well-stocked storehouse of creativity deep in the minds of the kids who belong to the city's Anti-Graffiti Network.

From it flows an almost-limitless supply of ideas for murals and paintings that now grace the walls of abandoned buildings and underpasses throughout the city.

These works of youthful art have turned gray and dingy surfaces into eye-pleasing scenes, with images such as waterfalls, sailboats at sea, forest scenes and similar sights not encountered in the drab city streets.

They also have instilled in the budding artists, many of whom are former graffiti scrawlers, a sense of pride that comes from the birth and execution of artistic ideas.

"Every time I look at one of my paintings," said Greg Turner, 18, "I think someone else has done it, because people go crazy over it."

Turner is just one of about 20 members of the Anti-Graffiti Network whose individual works, plus several mural-size paintings done by two or more of the group, are on exhibit through April at the Free Library's main branch on Logan Square in Center City.

Turner not only helped out with a few of the murals in the show, but has eight of his own works on display, including one colorful impression of Hong Kong harbor and another of an Indian temple.

Other themes run the gamut from abstract impressions of still-life figures to pastoral pastels of tropical islands boasting a single palm tree beneath a setting sun.

Many of the teens in the program still view exterior walls as nothing more than inner-city canvases waiting for some color. However, since they've joined the network, their spray-painting attacks are now done in conjunction with the community where the brick or cement walls stand.

"I used to write on walls," said Billy Leach, 15. "But not anymore. Since last summer I've worked on painting murals, and I've done my own paintings, too. My art teacher recommended me to the (anti-graffiti) program. If I wasn't in this, I'd probably still be out writing on walls."

Leach's painting, *Figure Study*, is on display at the library.

Young artists beautify city walls.

It captures with sensitivity and warmth the image of a man deep in thought at his desk. It's Leach's first painting to be displayed in a formal setting, and the idea of someone actually standing back and admiring his work, he said, has made him decide on a career in commercial art.

But you don't have to be a wall-scribbler to join the network. The only criteria are an interest in art and a desire to do something for the community.

Darnell Powell, 17, who says she has never defaced a wall with spray paint or anything else, is just as proud of her black-and-white abstract piece she calls "The Thinker" as Leach is about his art.

Her work, she said, was inspired by Richard Wright's novel *Native Son*.

It is a haunting, angular painting of a man's face that stares back at viewers with square, sad eyes that seem to be contemplating his life.

Powell says she didn't even realize she had a talent for painting until she joined the Anti-Graffiti Network two years ago.

"It's like something inside of me just started coming out," she said. "Like the abstract shapes. When I draw them, it's very peaceful."

According to Jane Golden, artistic director for the mural program, the participants have painted more than 600 murals over the past five years.

"We've done them from small walls to the sides of four-story buildings," she said.

The network is usually contacted through someone in the community who wants work done on a particular wall, or the wall is picked by the network, which, in turn, works with people in the surrounding area in regard to ideas for the wall.

The network was started by Mayor Goode in 1984 to combat the proliferation of graffiti that scarred walls all across the city.

Golden said that many of the murals are of quiet, relaxing scenes such as waterfalls and deer wandering in a forest because that's what the people want.

And the Anti-Graffiti Network is more than willing to oblige.

FROM

Maniac Magee

By
Jerry Spinelli

Illustrated by
Ken Spengler

For most of his life, Jeffrey Lionel Magee had a home. But when his parents died and his life changed, he had to learn to survive on his own. In the city of Two Mills, Jeffrey meets Amanda Beale, a friend who might be able to help him with his problem. But Two Mills has some special problems of its own, and "Maniac" Magee finds himself in the middle of them.

The town was buzzing. The schools were buzzing. Hallways. Lunchrooms. Streets. Playgrounds.

West End. East End.

Buzzing about the new kid in town. The stranger kid. Scraggly. Carrying a book. Flap-soled sneakers.

The kid who intercepted Brian Denehy's pass to Hands Down and punted it back longer than Denehy himself ever threw it.

The kid who rescued Arnold Jones from Finsterwald's backyard.

The kid who tattooed Giant John McNab's fastball for half a dozen home runs, then circled the sacks on a bunted frog.

Nobody knows who said it first, but somebody must have: "Kid's gotta be a maniac."

And somebody else must have said: "Yeah, reg'lar maniac."

And somebody else: "Yeah."

And that was it. Nobody (except Amanda Beale) had any other name for him, so pretty soon, when they wanted to talk about the new kid, that's what they called him: Maniac.

The legend had a name.

But not an address. At least, not an official one, with numbers.

What he did have was the deer shed at the Elmwood Park Zoo, which is where he slept his first few nights in town. What the deer ate, especially the carrots, apples, and day-old hamburger buns, he ate.

He started reading Amanda Beale's book his second day in town and finished it that afternoon. Ordinarily, he would have returned it immediately, but he was so fascinated by the story of the Children's Crusade that he kept it and read it the next day. And the next.

When he wasn't reading, he was wandering. When most people wander, they walk. Maniac Magee ran. Around town, around the nearby townships, always carrying the book, keeping it in perfect condition.

This is what he was doing when his life, as it often seemed to do, took an unexpected turn.

John McNab had never in his life met a kid he couldn't strike out. Until the runt. Now, as he thought about it, he came to two conclusions:

1. He couldn't stand having this blemish on his record.

2. If you beat a kid up, it's the same as striking him out.

So McNab and his pals went looking for the kid. They called themselves the Cobras. Nobody messed with them. At least, nobody in the West End.

The Cobras had heard that the kid hung around the park and the tracks, and that's where they spotted him one Saturday afternoon, on the tracks by the path that ran from the Oriole Street dead end to the park. He was down by Red Hill and heading away from them, book in hand, as usual.

But the Cobras just stood there, stunned.

"I don't believe it," one Cobra said.

"Must be a trick," said another.

"I heard about it," said another, "but I didn't believe it."

It wasn't a trick. It was true. The kid was *running* on the rail.

McNab scooped up a handful of track stones. He launched one. He snarled, "He's dead. Let's get 'im."

By the time Maniac looked back, they were almost on him. He wobbled once, leaped from the rail to the ground, and took off. He was at the Oriole Street dead end, but his instincts said no, not the street, too much open space. He stuck with the tracks. Coming into view above him was the house on Rako Hill, where he had eaten spaghetti. He could go there, to the whistling mother, the other kids, be safe. They wouldn't follow him in there. Would they?

Stones clanked off the steel rails. He darted left, skirted the dump, wove through the miniature mountain range of stone piles and into the trees . . . skiing on his heels down the steep bank and into the creek, frogs plopping, no time to look for stepping rocks . . . yells behind him now, war whoops, stones pelting the water, stinging his back . . . ah, the other side, through the trees and picker bushes, past the armory jeeps and out to the park boulevard, past the Italian restaurant on the corner, the bakery, screeching tires, row houses, streets, alleys, cars, porches, windows, faces staring, faces, faces . . .

the town whizzing past Maniac, a blur of faces, each face staring from its own window, each face in its own personal frame, its own house, its own address, someplace to be when there was no other place to be, how lucky to be a face staring out from a window . . .

And then—could it be?—the voices behind him were growing faint. He slowed, turned, stopped. They were lined up at a street a block back. They were still yelling and shaking their fists, but they weren't moving off the curb. And now they were laughing. Why were they laughing?

The Cobras were standing at Hector Street. Hector Street was the boundary between the East and West Ends. Or, to put it another way, between the blacks and whites. Not that you never saw a white in the East End or a black in the West End. People did cross the line now and then, especially if they were adults, and it was daylight.

But nighttime, forget it. And if you were a kid, day *or* night, forget it. Unless you had business on the other side, such as a sports team or school. But don't be just *strolling* along, as if you *belonged* there, as if you weren't *afraid*, as if you didn't even *notice* you were a different color from everybody around you.

The Cobras were laughing because they figured the dumb, scraggly runt would get out of the East End in about as good shape as a bare big toe in a convention of snapping turtles.

Of course, Maniac didn't know any of that. He was simply glad the chase was over. He turned and started walking, catching his breath.

East Chestnut. East Marshall. Green Street. Arch Street. He had been around here before. That first day with the girl named Amanda, other days jogging through. But this was Saturday, not a school day, and there was something different about the streets—kids. All over.

One of them jumped down from a front step and planted himself right in front of Maniac. Maniac had to jerk to a stop to keep from plowing into the kid. Even so, their noses were practically touching.

Maniac blinked and stepped back. The kid stepped forward. Each time Maniac stepped back, the kid stepped forward. They traveled practically half a block that way. Finally Maniac turned and started walking. The kid jumped around and plunked himself in front again. He bit off a chunk of the candy bar he was holding. "Where *you* goin'?" he said. Candy bar flakes flew from his mouth.

"I'm looking for Sycamore Street," said Maniac. "Do you know where it is?"

"Yeah, I know where it is."

Maniac waited, but the kid said nothing more. "Well, uh, do you think you could tell me where it is?"

Stone was softer than the kid's glare. "No."

Maniac looked around. Other kids had stopped playing, were staring.

Someone called: "Do 'im, Mars!"

Someone else: "Waste 'im!"

The kid, as you probably guessed by now, was none other than Mars Bar Thompson. Mars Bar heard the calls, and the stone got harder. Then suddenly he stopped glaring, suddenly he was smiling. He held up the candy bar, an inch from Maniac's lips. "Wanna bite?"

Maniac couldn't figure. "You sure?"

"Yeah, go ahead. Take a bite."

Maniac shrugged, took the Mars Bar, bit off a chunk, and handed it back. "Thanks."

Dead silence along the street. The kid had done the unthinkable, he had chomped on one of Mars's own bars. Not only that, but white kids just didn't put their mouths where black kids had had theirs, be it soda bottles, spoons, or candy bars. And the kid hadn't even gone for the unused end; he had chomped right over Mars Bar's own bite marks.

Mars Bar was confused. Who *was* this kid? *What* was this kid?

As usual, when Mars Bar got confused, he got mad. He thumped Maniac in the chest. "You think you bad or somethin'?"

Maniac, who was now twice as confused as Mars Bar, blinked. "Huh?"

"You think you come down here and be bad? That what you think?" Mars Bar was practically shouting now.

"No," said Maniac, "I don't think I'm bad. I'm not saying I'm an angel, either. Not even real good. Somewhere in between, I guess."

Mars Bar jammed his arms downward, stuck out his chin, and sneered. "Am I bad?"

Maniac was befuddled. "*I* don't know. One minute you're yelling at me, the next minute you're giving me a bite of your candy bar."

The chin jutted out more. "Tell me I'm bad."

Maniac didn't answer. Flies stopped buzzing.

"I said, tell me I'm bad."

Maniac blinked, shrugged, sighed. "It's none of my business. If you're bad, let your mother or father tell you."

Now it was Mars Bar doing the blinking, stepping back, trying to sort things out. After a while he looked down. "What's that?"

Before Maniac answered, "A book," Mars Bar had snatched it from his hand. "This ain't yours," he said. He flipped through some pages. "Looks like mine."

"It's somebody else's."

"It's mine. I'm keepin' it."

With rattlesnake speed, Maniac snatched the book back—except for one page, which stayed, ripped, in Mars Bar's hand.

"Give me the page," said Maniac.

Mars Bar grinned. "Take it, fishbelly."

Silence. Eyes. The flies were waiting. East End vultures.

Suddenly neither kid could see the other, because a broom came down like a straw curtain between their faces, and a voice said, "*I'll* take it."

It was the lady from the nearest house, out to sweep her steps. She lowered the broom but kept it between them. "Better yet," she said to Mars Bar, "just give it back to him."

Mars Bar glared up at her. There wasn't an eleven-year-old in the East End who could stand up to Mars Bar's glare. In the West End, even high-schoolers were known to crumble under the glare. To old ladies on both sides of Hector Street, it was all but fatal. And when Mars Bar stepped off a curb and combined the glare with his super-slow dip-stride slumpshuffle, well, it was said he could back up traffic all the way to Bridgeport while he took ten minutes to cross the street.

But not this time. This time Mars Bar was up against an East End lady in her prime, and she was matching him eyeball for eyeball. And when it was over, only one glare was left standing, and it wasn't Mars Bar's.

Mars Bar handed back the torn page, but not before he crumpled it into a ball. The broom pushed him away, turned him around, and swept him up the street.

The lady looked down at Maniac. A little of the glare lingered in her eyes. "You better get on, boy, where you belong. I can't be following you around. I got things to do."

Maniac just stood there a minute. There was something he felt like doing, and maybe he would have, but the lady turned and went back inside her house and shut the door. So he walked away.

Now what?

Maniac uncrumpled the page, flattened it out as best he could. How could he return the book to Amanda in this condition? He couldn't. But he had to. It was hers. Judging from that morning, she was pretty finicky about her books. What would make her madder—to not get the book back at all, or to get it back with a page ripped out? Maniac cringed at both prospects.

He wandered around the East End, jogging slowly, in no hurry now to find 728 Sycamore Street.

He was passing a vacant lot when he heard an all-too-familiar voice: "Hey, fishbelly!" He stopped, turned. This time Mars Bar wasn't alone. A handful of other kids trailed him down the sidewalk.

Maniac waited.

Coming up to him, Mars Bar said, "Where you runnin', boy?"

"Nowhere."

"You runnin' from us. You afraid."

"No, I just like to run."

"You wanna run?" Mars Bar grinned. "Go ahead. We'll give you a head start."

Maniac grinned back. "No thanks."

Mars Bar held out his hand. "Gimme my book."

Maniac shook his head.

Mars Bar glared. "Gimme it."

Maniac shook his head.

Mars Bar reached for it. Maniac pulled it away.

They moved in on him now. They backed him up. Some high-schoolers were playing basketball up the street, but they weren't noticing. And there wasn't a broom-swinging lady in sight. Maniac felt a hard flatness against his back. Suddenly his world was very small and very simple: a brick wall behind him, a row of scowling faces in front of him. He clutched the book with both hands. The faces were closing in. A voice called: "That you, Jeffrey?"

The faces parted. At the curb was a girl on a bike—Amanda! She hoisted the bike to the sidewalk and walked it over. She looked at the book, at the torn page. "Who ripped my book?"

Mars Bar pointed at Maniac. "He did."

Amanda knew better. "*You* ripped my book."

Mars Bar's eyes went big as headlights. "I did *not*!"

"You *did*. You lie."

"I *didn't*!"

"You *did*!" She let the bike fall to Maniac. She grabbed the book and started kicking Mars Bar in his beloved sneakers. "I got a little brother and a little sister that crayon all over my books, and I got a dog that eats them and poops on them and that's just inside my own family, and I'm *not*—gonna have *nobody*—else *messin'*—with my *books*! You under-*stand*?"

By then Mars Bar was hauling on up the street past the basketball players, who were rolling on the asphalt with laughter.

Amanda took the torn page from Maniac. To her, it was the broken wing of a bird, a pet out in the rain. She turned misty eyes to Maniac. "It's one of my favorite pages."

Maniac smiled. "We can fix it."

The way he said it, she believed. "Want to come to my house?" she said.

"Sure," he said.

When they walked in, Amanda's mother was busy with her usual tools: a yellow plastic bucket and a sponge. She was scrubbing pur-ple crayon off the TV screen.

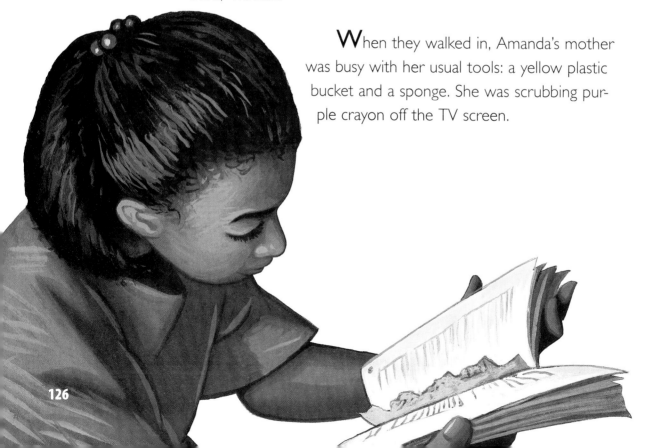

"Mom," said Amanda, "this is Jeffrey—" She whispered, "What's your last name?"

He whispered, "Magee."

She said, "Magee."

Mrs. Beale held up a hand, said, "Hold it," and went on scrubbing. When she finally finished, she straightened up, turned, and said, "Now, what?"

"Mom, this is Jeffrey Magee. You know."

Amanda was hardly finished when Maniac zipped across the room and stuck out his hand. "Nice to meet you, Mrs. . . . Mrs. . . ."

"Beale."

"Mrs. Beale."

They shook hands. Mrs. Beale smiled. "So you're the book boy." She started nodding. "Manda came home one day— 'Mom, there's a boy I loaned one of my books to!' 'Loaned a *book*? *You*?' 'Mom, he practically *made* me. He really likes books. I met him on—' "

"Mo-om!" Amanda screeched. "I never said all *that*!"

Mrs. Beale nodded solemnly—"No, of course you didn't"—and gave Maniac a huge wink, which made Amanda screech louder, until something crashed in the kitchen. Mrs. Beale ran. Amanda and Maniac ran.

The scene in the kitchen stopped them cold: one little girl, eyes wide, standing on a countertop; one little boy, eyes wide, standing just below her on a chair; one shattered glass jar and some stringy pale-colored glop on the floor; one growing cloud of sauerkraut fumes.

The girl was Hester, age four; the boy was Lester, age three. In less than five minutes, while Mrs. Beale and Amanda cleaned up the floor, Hester and Lester and their dog Bow Wow were in the backyard wrestling and tickling and jumping and just generally going wild with their new buddy—and victim—Maniac Magee.

Maniac was still there when Mr. Beale came home from his Saturday shift at the tire factory.

He was there for dinner, when Hester and Lester pushed their chairs alongside his.

He was there to help Amanda mend her torn book.

He was there watching TV afterward, with Hester riding one knee, Lester the other.

He was there when Hester and Lester came screaming down the stairs with a book, Amanda screaming even louder after them, the kids shoving the book and themselves onto Maniac's lap, Amanda finally calming down because they didn't want to crayon the book, they only wanted Maniac to read. And so he read *Lyle, Lyle, Crocodile* to Hester and Lester and, even though they pretended not to listen, to Amanda and Mr. and Mrs. Beale.

And he was there when Hester and Lester were herded upstairs to bed, and Mrs. Beale said, "Don't you think it's about time you're heading home, Jeffrey? Your parents'll be wondering."

So Maniac, wanting to say something but not knowing how, got into the car for Mr. Beale to drive him home. And then he made his mistake. He waited for only two or three blocks to go by before saying to Mr. Beale, "This is it."

Mr. Beale stopped, but he didn't let Maniac out of the car. He looked at him funny. Mr. Beale knew what his passenger apparently didn't: East End was East End and West End was West End, and the house this white lad was pointing to was filled with black people, just like every other house on up to Hector Street.

Mr. Beale pointed this out to Maniac. Maniac's lip started to quiver, and right there, with the car idling in the middle of the street, Maniac told him that he didn't really have a home, unless you counted the deer shed at the zoo.

Mr. Beale made a U-turn right there and headed back. Only Mrs. Beale was still downstairs when they walked into the house. She listened to no more than ten seconds' worth of Mr. Beale's explanation before saying to Maniac, "You're staying here."

Not long after, Maniac was lying in Amanda's bed, Amanda having been carried over to Hester and Lester's room, where she often slept anyway.

Before Maniac could go to sleep, however, there was something he had to do. He flipped off the covers and went downstairs. Before the puzzled faces of Mr. and Mrs. Beale, he opened the front door and looked at the three cast-iron digits nailed to the door frame: seven two eight. He kept staring at them, smiling. Then he closed the door, said a cheerful "Goodnight," and went back to bed.

Maniac Magee finally had an address.

How to
Make an Action Plan

Work to get something *changed* in your community.

Making an action plan is one way to bring about community improvement. An action plan is a written proposal, stating what it is the writer wants to do, why he or she wants to do it, and how it can be done. The proposal should also include evidence that supports the writer's position. This evidence can be photos, articles, and surveys. Together, the proposal and the evidence make up an action plan.

Dear Mayor
I would like a baseball
field built in the
space

BOSTON ST.

BLEACHERS

BLEACHERS

WHITFIELD ST.

SPORTS

another cha

1 Choose and Support an Issue

What is one thing in your community you want to change? Check out local news reports to see what other people think your community needs. Pick an issue you feel strongly about, but not one that's too big to tackle. Perhaps you feel that your neighborhood needs a dog run where dogs can exercise safely or that your community needs a new public softball diamond. If you did a needs assessment survey, you may want to use that issue. Write a short proposal telling about your idea.

Once you choose an issue, collect evidence to support your idea. Start a file of newspaper clippings. As you collect information, take notes. Support for your position can come from many sources. Talk to people you know. They may be willing to sign a petition or write letters in support of your idea. Local or national newspapers, TV stations, and radio shows may have covered your issue.

TOOLS

- paper and pen

- markers, crayons, or pencils

- folder

- camera (optional)

2 Making a Plan

Any good action plan includes ideas for how the plan might work. For example, if you think your community needs a public dog run, you might find out how much land must be set aside for it. You might research available public areas. You may want to include information about how much the project is likely to cost the community.

Decide what information you need to explain how your idea could work. Then, research that information.

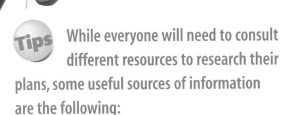

Tips While everyone will need to consult different resources to research their plans, some useful sources of information are the following:
- local Historical Society
- school or public library
- City Hall
- Chamber of Commerce

How Am I Doing?

Before you begin your action plan, take a minute to ask yourself these questions:

- Can you state the idea for your action plan briefly and clearly?

- Do you have at least three pieces of evidence that support your idea?

- Have you collected enough information to explain how the idea could work?

3 Write Your Action Plan

Write a proposal for action. Begin by briefly stating what it is that you want to build or change. Continue the proposal by giving at least three reasons explaining why your idea is a sound one. Finally, explain how the idea might be put into action. Be sure to list the evidence you have collected to support your idea and to show how it could work. Reread your proposal to be sure that it is clear and complete.

If You Are Using a Computer . . .

Draft your action proposal using the Report format. Then write the letter for your proposal in the Letter format. Create your own stationery by choosing from the selection of letterheads.

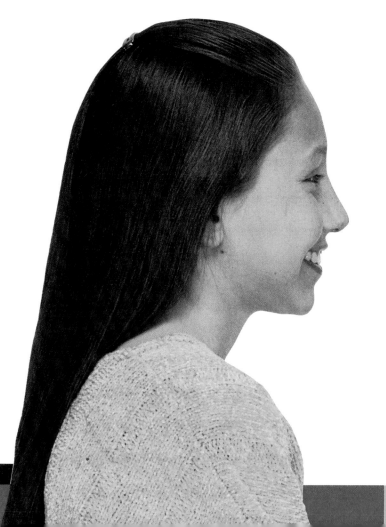

4 Present Your Action Plan

Now it's time to put your action plan together. Put your proposal in the left-hand pocket of your folder. Gather together all of the evidence you have collected. Put the evidence in the right-hand side of the folder. Are you going to mail your action plan to the mayor or a community leader? Write a brief letter stating your idea and explaining that you have included an action plan to describe the idea in detail. Put everything in a mailing envelope and address it clearly and neatly. Include a self-addressed, stamped envelope so the material will be returned to you. Remember to keep a copy of the letter and evidence for yourself. You might want to put your copy of the action plan on display in your classroom.

CONGRATULATIONS

Now you know what an urban planner does. Next time you're in a city, think about all the planning that's needed to make things run.

Karen Heit
Urban Planner ▶

Glossary

al·ley
(al′ē) *noun*
Narrow passageway behind or between buildings.

ar·mory
(är′mə rē) *noun*
Place where weapons are stored.

bi·o·de·grad·a·ble
(bī′ō di grā′də bəl) *adjective*
Something that decays easily and naturally with the help of living organisms like bacteria.

bou·le·vard
(bŏŏl′ə värd) *noun*
A wide city street.

bound·a·ry
(boun′də rē) *noun*
A line or other thing that marks a border or limit.

ca·ble car
(kā′bəl kär′) *noun*
A railroad car pulled along the rails by an underground cable.

can·ti·le·ver bridge
(kan′tl ē′vər brij) *noun*
A cantilever is a structure, supported at one end, that is anchored to a wall or a pier. A cantilever bridge is a bridge whose span is formed by two cantilevers projecting toward each other, sometimes with an extra section between them.

con·ven·ience
(kən vēn′yəns) *noun*
Anything that makes work easier or adds to one's comfort.

dead end
(ded end) *noun*
A street that has only one way to enter or exit.

de·faced (di fāst′) *verb*
Spoiled or hurt the looks of. He *defaced* the property. ▲ deface

cable car

136

de·fi·ance
(di fī′ əns) *noun*
A resistance to authority or to any opposing force.

de·mol·ish·ing
(di mol′ish ing) *verb*
Tearing down or destroying. ▲ **demolish**

dis·ap·pear·ed
(dis′ə pērd′) *verb*
Stopped being seen. Vanished; went away.
▲ **disappear**

Thesaurus
disappeared
dissolved
eclipsed
melted away

dump·sters
(dump′stərs) *noun*
Large, metal trash bins.
▲ **dumpster**

en·dures
(en dŏŏrz′) *verb*
Continues, or lasts, for a long time. Something that is taken care of *endures* longer than something that is abused. ▲ **endure**

en·vi·ron·ment
(en vī′rən mənt) *noun*
All the things, such as air, water, minerals, animals, plants, and people, that surround one or more living things.

hab·i·tats
(hab′i tats′) *noun*
Places where animals or plants naturally live and grow. ▲ **habitat**

ha·rass·ing
(hə ras′ing) *verb*
Bothering or troubling over and over again. ▲ **harass**

Fact File

Over 70% of our trash ends up in landfills.

in·ter·sec·tions
(in′tər sək′shəns) *noun*
Places where two or more things cross each other.
▲ **intersection**

intersections

land·fills
(land′filz′) *noun*
Areas of land that have been filled in with garbage and covered with layers of dirt. ▲ **landfill**

a	add	ŏŏ	took	ə =
ā	ace	ōō	pool	a in *above*
â	care	u	up	e in *sicken*
ä	palm	û	burn	i in *possible*
e	end	yōō	fuse	o in *melon*
ē	equal	oi	oil	u in *circus*
i	it	ou	pout	
ī	ice	ng	ring	
o	odd	th	thin	
ō	open	ŧh	this	
ô	order	zh	vision	

Glossary

pier

land·mark
(land′märk) *noun*
An easily seen object, such as a building, tree, or statue, that helps one to find or recognize a place.

ped·dler (ped′ lər) *noun*
A person who sells things from door to door or from a cart or stand on the street. We each bought an apple from the *peddler*.

pier (pēr) *noun*
A structure built out over water on posts, used as a landing place for ships.

pre·dic·a·ment
(pri dik′ə mənt) *noun*
A difficult or troubling situation.

push·cart
(poŏsh′kärt′) *noun*
A light cart on wheels that can be pushed by hand.

reck·less
(rek′lis) *adjective*
Not careful.

row hou·ses
(rō houz′es) *noun*
A series of houses in which neighboring units share a wall. ▲ **row house**

sar·cas·tic
(sär kas′tik) *adjective*
Witty, in a mean way; meant to hurt or humiliate.

sew•age (sōō′ ij) *noun*
Waste that is carried off
from sinks, toilets, and
other devices by sewers
and drains.

sin•gle-mind•ed
(sing′gəl mīn′did)
adjective
Having only one aim or
purpose.

sour•dough
(souər′ dō′) *adjective*
Made from a type of
dough that contains an
actively fermenting yeast.
San Francisco is known for
its *sourdough* bread.

stuck-up
(stuk′ up′) *adjective*
Snobbish or conceited.

sur•veil•lance
(sər vā′lens) *noun*
Close observation.

sus•pen•sion bridge
(sə spen′shən brij) *noun*
A bridge held up by large
cables or chains that are
strung between a series
of towers.

Fact File

The longest suspension
bridge in the world is the
Akashi-Kaiko bridge in Japan,
which spans 6,496 feet!

town•ship
(toun′ship) *noun*
A division of a county,
which has local powers of
government over schools,
roads, and other aspects of
the community.

traf•fic co•or•di•na•tion
(traf′ik kō ôr′dnā′shən)
noun
The planning of
vehicle movement in a
populated area.

truss bridge
(trus′ brij′) *noun*
A bridge held up by a
framework of beams or rods.

ur•ban
(ûr′bən) *adjective*
Of, living in, or having to
do with a city.

van•dals (van′dlz) *noun*
People who destroy or
damage things on purpose,
especially works of art or
public property. ▲ **vandal**

ve•hi•cles
(vē′i kəlz) *noun*
A means of carrying people
or things, especially over
land, sea, or air. Subway
trains are efficient *vehicles*
for carrying large numbers
of people through cities.
▲ **vehicle**

a	add	ŏŏ	took	ə =
ā	ace	ōō	pool	a in *above*
â	care	u	up	e in *sicken*
ä	palm	û	burn	i in *possible*
e	end	yōō	fuse	o in *melon*
ē	equal	oi	oil	u in *circus*
i	it	ou	pout	
ī	ice	ng	ring	
o	odd	th	thin	
ō	open	th	this	
ô	order	zh	vision	

suspension bridge

Authors & Illustrators

Tricia Brown *pages 10–21*

Tricia Brown has traveled throughout Latin America and Southeast Asia, but she is always glad to return home to San Francisco. She is well known for the photo essays she has written about kids in different California neighborhoods. *The City by the Bay* is special to her because she wrote it to help the people of her hometown. Brown donates her earnings from the book to organizations that help children in San Francisco.

Peter Collington *pages 94–113*

Peter Collington's career in picture books began with *Little Pickle*, a book that grew from pictures he had drawn to amuse his small daughter. *The Coming of the Surfman* is also a first for Collington—his first book with words. All of his other books have been wordless fantasy stories.

Jean Merrill *pages 54–69*

Since 1951, Jean Merrill has written more than 20 books for kids, but *The Pushcart War* is probably her most famous book. This city tale has been made into a television play and was also performed on the stage and on the radio. Surprisingly, Merrill lives in the country. She grew up on a farm and loved to spend time out of doors. "Books were the only things that could keep me indoors," Merrill says.

Jerry Spinelli *pages 116–129*

When he was sixteen years old, Jerry Spinelli dreamed of being a major-league shortstop. Then his high school football team in Norristown, Pennsylvania, won a big game. Swept up in the excitement of the event, Spinelli wrote a poem about it. A local paper published the poem, and Spinelli has been writing ever since.

"Experiences are not really complete until I write about them."

Walt Whitman *page 46*

Although his writing was first published over one hundred years ago, Walt Whitman's words still ring true today. Born in 1819, Whitman did not start writing poetry until he was thirty years old. At that time, he took his first trip to New Orleans, Louisiana. The people and places he saw there inspired him. By 1855, Whitman had written enough poetry to put together a collection called *Leaves of Grass*, which he published himself. Today, *Leaves of Grass* remains Whitman's most popular book.

Vera B. Williams *pages 26–45*

This author/illustrator grew up in the Bronx, but considered all of New York City to be her neighborhood. Her family walked everywhere, rode ferries, ice-skated in public parks, and visited city libraries. One of Williams' childhood paintings was included in an exhibit at New York's Museum of Modern Art. Williams said she was "thrilled to be a citizen of so grand a place as New York City."

Books &

Author Study

Walt Whitman

I Hear America Singing
by Walt Whitman
illustrated by Robert Subuda
In his most famous poem, Whitman celebrates America and its people.

Walt Whitman
by Catherine Reef
This biography includes photos of Walt Whitman, along with excerpts from his poems and other writings.

Walt Whitman

Fiction

A Girl Called Al
by Constance Greene
Two girls who live in the same city apartment building become best friends, sharing good times and bad.

The Great Smith House Hustle
by Jane Louise Curry
Cisco and Poppy Smith have just moved to Pittsburgh, where they've stumbled on a mystery that threatens their community. With the help of friends and neighbors, they may be able to solve it.

Mop, Moondance and the Nagasaki Knights
by Walter Dean Myers
T.J. and his friends love the city park where they play baseball. But they soon discover that for some people, the park is a place to live.

Nonfiction

City! San Francisco
by Shirley Climo
photographs by George Ancona
Climo and Ancona take their readers on a tour of a great California city.

The Building of Manhattan
by Donald A. Mackay
In this carefully researched book, Mackay uses words and pictures to show how New York has grown since its beginnings as a Dutch colony over 300 years ago.

The Great Fire
by Jim Murphy
Newspapers described the Chicago fire of 1871 as the great calamity of the age. This book puts readers in the middle of one of the most devastating fires in U.S. history.

xMedia

Videos

Daniel and the Towers
Public Media Video
Daniel, a Los Angeles boy, helps a street artist build a beautiful tower out of old junk, in this story based on a real event. (55 minutes)

Recycling
Library Video Series
All across the United States young people are improving the quality of life in their communities by working on recycling projects. In this video, you'll meet some of these real-life environmental heroes. (26 minutes)

Taking Care of Terrific
WonderWorks
Family Movie Series
On their daily journeys to the Boston Common, a small boy named Terrific and his teenaged baby-sitter meet with interesting characters and incredible adventures. (58 minutes)

Software

Decisions, Decisions: Urbanization
Tom Snyder Productions
You're the mayor of Alpine, and you must decide how your community will grow.

Immigrant: The Irish Experience in Boston
Wings/Sunburst
Many immigrants came from Ireland to Boston in the 1800s. This program allows you to join one such family and to make the same kinds of decisions that real-life Irish immigrants had to face.

MacUSA
Broderbund
Go on-line and use this atlas to learn about cities in all 50 states and in Puerto Rico. The atlas includes facts, pictures, and terrific maps.

Magazines

3-2-1 Contact
Children's Television Workshop
This science and technology magazine often includes articles about how technology helps solve city problems.

Scholastic News
Scholastic Inc.
Articles in this classroom news magazine focus on current events that affect kids from a variety of cities.

A Place to Write

How can you help your neighborhood? For information about publications and activities in your area, write to

United Neighborhood Centers of America, Inc.
4801 Massachusetts
 Ave. NW
Washington, D.C.
20016

Acknowledgments

Grateful acknowledgment is made to the following sources for permission to reprint from previously published material. The publisher has made diligent efforts to trace the ownership of all copyrighted material in this volume and believes that all necessary permissions have been secured. If any errors or omissions have inadvertently been made, proper corrections will gladly be made in future editions.

Cover: © "Looking Along Broadway Towards Grace Church," 1981, Red Grooms, Marlborough Gallery.

Interior: Selections and cover from THE CITY BY THE BAY published by Chronicle Books, San Francisco. Copyright © 1993 by The Junior League of San Francisco, Inc. Written by Tricia Brown and The Junior League of San Francisco, illustrated by Elisa Kleven. Reprinted by permission.

Text, art, and cover from SCOOTER by Vera B. Williams. Copyright © 1993 by Vera B. Williams. Reprinted by permission of Greenwillow Books, a division of William Morrow & Company, Inc.

Selection from BACK TO THE CITY: PITTSBURGH! Copyright © 1992 NeighborFair Pittsburgh Inc. Used by permission.

Selection from THE PUSHCART WAR by Jean Merrill. Text copyright © 1964 by Jean Merrill. Reprinted by permission of HarperCollins Publishers. Cover illustration by Carl Cassler. Cover illustration copyright © by Carl Cassler. Used by permission of Dell Books, a division of Bantam Doubleday Dell Publishing Group, Inc.

Selection and cover from GARBAGE! by Evan and Janet Hadingham. Copyright © 1990 by Evan and Janet Hadingham and WGBH Educational Foundation. Reprinted by permission of Simon & Schuster Books for Young Readers, Simon & Schuster Children's Publishing Division.

"50 Can-Do Kids" by Kathy Love. Reprinted from the March 1993 issue of RANGER RICK® magazine with the permission of the publisher, the National Wildlife Federation. Copyright © 1993 by the National Wildlife Federation.

"Cornerstone Pool Customer Satisfaction Survey" used by permission of the Town of West Hartford, CT, Department of Leisure Services .

"The Coming of the Surfman" from THE COMING OF THE SURFMAN by Peter Collington. Copyright © 1993 by Peter Collington. Originally published in Great Britain in 1993 by Jonathan Cape Ltd., an imprint of Random House UK Ltd. Reprinted by permission of Alfred A. Knopf, Inc.

"Art Show Draws Upon Ex-Graffiti Scrawlers" from *Philadelphia Daily News*, March 29, 1989, p. 14. Reprinted by permission of Knight-Ridder Tribune News Service.

Selection and cover from MANIAC MAGEE by Jerry Spinelli. Copyright © 1990 by Jerry Spinelli. By permission of Little, Brown & Company.

Cover from CITIES: CITIZENS & CIVILIZATIONS by Fiona Macdonald, illustrated by John James. Illustration copyright © 1992 by The Salariya Book Co. Ltd. Published by Franklin Watts.

Cover from A JAR OF DREAMS by Yoshiko Uchida, illustrated by Kuniko Craft. Illustration copyright © 1981 by Kuniko Craft. Published by Atheneum Books for Young Readers, Simon & Schuster Children's Publishing Division.

Cover from TAILS OF THE BRONX by Jill Pinkwater, illustrated by Brian Pinkney. Cover illustration copyright © 1991 by Brian Pinkney. Published by Simon & Schuster Books for Young Readers, Simon & Schuster Children's Publishing Division.

Cover from WHERE THE RIVER RUNS by Nancy Price Graff, photograph by Richard Howard. Photograph copyright © 1993 by Richard Howard. Published by Little, Brown & Company.

Photography and Illustration Credits

Photos: © John Lei for Scholastic Inc., all Tool Box items unless otherwise noted. p. 2 bl: © John Lei for Scholastic Inc.; tl: © Maryellen Baker for Scholastic Inc.; cl: © Frank Cruz for Scholastic Inc. pp. 2-3 c: © Ann Summa for Scholastic Inc.; background: © Tom McHugh/Photo Researchers, Inc. p. 4 c: © Tony Freeman/PhotoEdit. p. 5 c: © Ana Esperanza Nance for Scholastic Inc. p. 6 c: © Tony Freeman/PhotoEdit. pp. 8-9 c: © *The City by the Golden Gate*, painting by Jane Wooster Scott/Superstock. p. 23 tl: © Richard Laird/FPG International Corp.; bl: © Rafael Macia, Photo Researchers, Inc.; tc: © J.D. Cuban/All Sport; bc: © Joseph Nettis/Photo Researchers, Inc.; br: © FPG International Corp.; tr: © Andre Jenny/Stock South Inc.; cl: © Rafael Macia/Photo Researchers, Inc. p. 24 c: © Alain Thomas/Photo Researchers, Inc.; tl: © Barry Durand/Odyssey Productions; Sears Tower: © Steve Elmore/Tom Stack & Associates; Zoo: © Robert Frerck/Tony Stone Worldwide; tc: © J.D. Cuban/All Sport; bc: © Hank Morgan/Photo Researchers, Inc.; c: Alain Thomas/Photo Researchers, Inc.; tr: © Steve DiPaola/All Sport; cr: © Ron Thomas/FPG International Corp.; br: © Bernard Wolff, Photo Researchers, Inc. p. 25 tl: © Sam C. Pierson, Jr./Photo Researchers, Inc.; bl: © Comstock, Inc.; tc: © Mike Powell/All Sport c: James Blank/Tony Stone Images; "HOLLYWOOD" sign: © Tom McHugh/Photo Researchers, Inc.; bc: © Whitby/NST/FPG International Corp.; tr: © David Bartruff/FPG International Corp.; cr: © Rich Buzzelli/Tom Stack & Associates; br: © Comstock Inc. pp. 46-47 c: © *Study for Grand Central* Red Grooms/Courtesy, Marlborough Gallery. pp. 48-49 bl: © NeighborFair Pittsburg, Inc. p. 51 bl: © Stanley Bach for Scholastic Inc.; br: © Ann Summa for Scholastic Inc. pp. 52-53 c: © Detail of *Union Square Station 1992* by Edith Kramer MTA Arts for Transit. p. 70 all: © Ann Summa for Scholastic Inc. p. 71 c: © Ann Summa for Scholastic Inc.; br: © Pete Saloutos/ The Stock Market. p. 72 all: © Ann Summa for Scholastic Inc. p. 73 cr, bl: © Ann Summa for Scholastic Inc.; tl: © Maryellen Baker for Scholastic Inc. pp. 74-75 c: The Bettmann Archive. p. 75 bl (rabbit): © Elwood H. Smith; cr: © John McGrail; br: © The Bettmann Archive. p. 76 tl: © Elwood H. Smith. p. 77 c, br: © The Bettmann Archive. p. 78 c, tl, br: © John McGrail; bl: © WGBH. p. 79 cr, bl: © John McGrail. p. 80 cl: © Elwood H. Smith. p. 81 cl, cr: © Elwood H. Smith. p. 82 bc: © WGBH. p. 81 tr: © Elwood H. Smith. pp. 84-85 © Paul Childress. p. 86-87 bc: © Paul Childress. p. 87 tl: © Paul Childress. pp. 88-89 © LuisCastañeda/The Image Bank. p. 89 c: © Stanley Bach for Scholastic Inc. p. 90 bl: © John Lei for Scholastic Inc.; bc, cl: © Stanley Bach for Scholastic Inc. p. 91 bl: © John Lei for Scholastic Inc.; br: © Ann Summa for Scholastic Inc. p. 115 cl: Courtesy of Anti-Graffiti Network. p. 131 all: © John Lei for Scholastic Inc. p. 132 br: © Stanley Bach for Scholastic Inc.; br: © John Lei for Scholastic Inc. pp. 134-135 c: © Stanley Bach for Scholastic Inc. p. 134 br: © John Lei for Scholastic Inc. p. 135 tr: © Stanley Bach for Scholastic Inc.; br: © Ann Summa for Scholastic Inc. p. 136 bl: © David Weintraub/Photo Researchers, Inc. p. 137 c: © Georg Gerster/Comstock, Inc. p. 138 © Frank Pedrick/The Image Works. p. 139 bl: © Snider/The Image Works. p. 140 tl: courtesy of Tricia Brown; cl: courtesy of Peter Collington; bl: courtesy of Jean Merrill; p. 140 tr: courtesy of Scholastic Trade Department; cr: The Bettmann Archive; br: courtesy of William Morrow & Company. p. 142 br: © M.E. Warren Photography/Photo Researchers, Inc.; bl: The Bettmann Archive. p. 143 br: © Stanley Bach for Scholastic Inc.

Illustrations: p. 22 t: Donna Ingemanson; pp. 22-25: Steven Stankiewicz; pp. 54-69: Beata Szpura; pp. 80-81: Elwood Smith; pp. 92-93: Andrew Boerger; pp. 114-115: Danuta Jarecka; pp. 116-129: Ken Spengler.